Cambridge Elements ≡

Elements in Second Language Acquisition
edited by
Alessandro Benati
The University of Hong Kong
John W. Schwieter
Wilfrid Laurier University, Ontario

GENERATIVE SECOND LANGUAGE ACQUISITION

Roumyana Slabakova
University of Southampton and NTNU Norwegian University of Science and Technology

Tania Leal
University of Nevada, Reno

Amber Dudley
University of Southampton

(with Micah Stack)
University of Nevada, Reno

CAMBRIDGE
UNIVERSITY PRESS

CAMBRIDGE
UNIVERSITY PRESS

University Printing House, Cambridge CB2 8BS, United Kingdom

One Liberty Plaza, 20th Floor, New York, NY 10006, USA

477 Williamstown Road, Port Melbourne, VIC 3207, Australia

314–321, 3rd Floor, Plot 3, Splendor Forum, Jasola District Centre,
New Delhi – 110025, India

79 Anson Road, #06–04/06, Singapore 079906

Cambridge University Press is part of the University of Cambridge.

It furthers the University's mission by disseminating knowledge in the pursuit of
education, learning, and research at the highest international levels of excellence.

www.cambridge.org
Information on this title: www.cambridge.org/9781108708227
DOI: 10.1017/9781108762380

© Roumyana Slabakova 2020

First published 2020

A catalogue record for this publication is available from the British Library.

ISBN 978-1-108-70822-7 Paperback
ISSN 2517-7974 (online)
ISSN 2517-7966 (print)

Generative Second Language Acquisition

Elements in Second Language Acquisition

DOI:10.1017/9781108762380
First published online: August 2020

Roumyana Slabakova
University of Southampton and NTNU Norwegian University of Science and Technology

Tania Leal
University of Nevada, Reno

Amber Dudley
University of Southampton

(with Micah Stack)
University of Nevada, Reno

Author for correspondence: Roumyana Slabakova, R.Slabakova@soton.ac.uk

Abstract: Most human beings grow up speaking more than one language; a lot of us also acquire an additional language or languages other than our mother tongue. This Element in the Second Language Acquisition series investigates the human capacity to learn additional languages later in life and introduces the seminal processes involved in this acquisition. The authors discuss how to analyze learner data and what the findings tell us about language learning; critically assessing a leading theory of how adults learn a second language: Generative SLA. This theory describes both universal innate knowledge and individual experiences as crucial for language acquisition. This Element makes the relevant connections between first and second language acquisition and explores whether they are fundamentally similar processes. Slabakova et al. provide fascinating pedagogical questions that encourage students and teachers to reflect upon the experiences of second language learners.

Keywords: generative linguistics, second language acquisition, input, language development, language teaching

ISBNs: 9781108708227 (PB), 9781108762380 (OC)
ISSNs: 2517-7974 (online), 2517-7966 (print)

Contents

1 What Are the Key Concepts?

1.1 What Does Generative Second Language Acquisition Try to Explain?

The scholarly field of second language acquisition (SLA) aims to explain the process through which people who already speak their mother tongue learn a second, third, and additional languages. SLA focuses mainly on adult learners – people who start learning the additional language after puberty. Related but separate fields of inquiry, such as bilingualism, child SLA, third language acquisition, heritage language acquisition, and instructed second and foreign language learning and teaching ask slightly different research questions. For the past sixty years, SLA has aimed to reveal and describe different facets of the SLA process.

A strength of the field is the variety of perspectives from which the process is examined. It is well established that the SLA process is embedded in a linguistic environment, happens in social situations, and depends on the culture of the societal group. Its path, rate, and accuracy may depend on a person's motivation, surroundings, and learning strategies. However, in spite of their individual circumstances, personal experiences, and native grammars, second language learners end up with a version of the second language grammar. If they didn't, speakers of that language wouldn't understand them. Thus, the most important research question informing language cognition is: How does knowledge of the additional language come to be in the speaker's mind so that they can understand and produce the phrases, sentences, and discourse of the new language? A central insight we advance in this Element is that, while learning a second language certainly depends on exposure to and usage of that language, universal language acquisition processes also lend a significant hand.

Because the SLA research endeavor is transdisciplinary and multifunctional, we can say that the generative approach to SLA (henceforth GenSLA) constitutes a substantial addition to the wide-ranging picture that the rest of SLA paints (Lee & Lardiere, 2019; Rothman & Slabakova, 2018; Slabakova, Leal, & Liskin-Gasparro, 2014, 2015; White, 2018a, 2018b). In this Element, we will focus on GenSLA as a specific approach to the cognitive investigation of learning an additional language, which means that we will predominantly focus on grammatical rather than sociolinguistic issues.

What can GenSLA contribute to SLA studies? Since its beginning in the 1980s, GenSLA has been successful at first identifying and then elucidating numerous puzzles in the SLA process (Adjemian, 1976; Flynn, 1985; Liceras, 1986; Schachter, 1988; White, 1989). For the most part, these puzzles are based on interesting distinctions in linguistic constructions or differences between languages. We give many examples in this introductory section. One of them is the acquisition of long-distance *wh*-questions in examples (6) and (7); another is the interpretation of null subjects as in examples (8) and (9). A major advantage of GenSLA is that it offers an independent and well-understood theoretical framework that can be used to study linguistic behavior. Like any cognitive scientific endeavor, GenSLA has experienced theory-internal development based on evolving linguistic concepts. As such, it has provided researchers with theory-based predictions informed by both linguistic and SLA theory. It has also guided research designs used to obtain experimental evidence documenting changes in behavior – that is, evidence of learning. This research agenda is now in its fifth decade and is still going strong. But let's start at the beginning by defining the most key concept of SLA.

1.2 What Is Language?

We assume a definition that views language from a cognitive and generative perspective: a system of signs and the rules governing how those signs combine; a grammar that generates all the acceptable sentences in a language while excluding unacceptable ones. A sign is a mapping of form and meaning. Knowledge of this system of signs lives in the human mind as a network of linguistic representations. A speaker of English knows unconsciously that *I saw the snake that bit me* is a good sentence, while *I the snake that bit me saw* is not, although they may still understand the message. English speakers recognize words (*snake, the, I*), the grammatical shape of words (*bit* is a past-tense form of *bite*), and the correct word order. Even though the same words participate in the second sentence, English speakers know intuitively that they are not in the proper order. English speakers also know what event in the real world this sentence is describing; they can attribute meaning to the sentence's form.

Linguists who embrace and study this view of language are called generative linguists. Why do we call this branch of linguistics *generative*? The term stems from the idea that sentences are *generated* rather than reproduced whole from some repository of ready-made sentences in the brain. Each time we convey a message, we start clothing our thoughts in language by putting the words together in ways we may have never heard before, checking their grammatical shapes, and then their order. We instinctively – and unconsciously – know whether the sentence we have just uttered sounds fine and whether it is appropriate in the discourse situation. We can monitor ourselves and correct slips of the tongue, if they happen. We can generate language!

1.3 How Do Children Acquire Language?

At the outset, it helps to think of the main elements of language structure separately: sounds, words, grammar, sentences. A remarkable fact about language acquisition is that, by the time they are born, children can already distinguish one sound from another. We know this because they react differently when they are habituated to one language sound, and suddenly hear another (Eimas et al., 1971). Infants are also sensitive to the language of their environment, since they have been exposed to it in the womb. Six-to-eight-month-old children typically pick out words and distinguish well-formed structure. By the time their first birthday comes around, infants know a lot about language! And it goes very quickly from there.

At around eighteen months, children experience a spurt of vocabulary growth (Bloom, 1973). They learn a few words every day, up to twenty a week. How do children know to narrow their search for names of objects? Psychologists propose that they are guided by innate constraints. One such constraint is known as Mutual Exclusivity: the assumption that each object in the world can only be referred to by a single name (Clark, 2009). If an object is labeled "brush," then another object that is unlike the first object must be called something else. In one study, researchers showed seventeen-month-old infants two objects and asked them to point to the "dax" (Halberda, 2003). One object, a brush, was known to the children, while the other was unfamiliar. The infants were able to point to the new referent as the "dax" after a single exposure. Fast mapping, along with new word-categorizing skills appears to underlie this astonishing vocabulary growth.

Linguists have made another important discovery: for children's lexicon to grow, language must be heard in sufficient quantity so that the brain can extract the necessary information from the linguistic stream. The amount and variety of language exposure has been thought to have consequences for children's subsequent language development and reading skills (Hoff & Naigles, 2002). For instance, reading to toddlers exposes them to a wider lexicon than everyday home communication. In addition, learning words and grammar are complementary and tightly knit processes. The amount and diversity of verbal stimulation fosters earlier and richer language outcomes, not just in terms of vocabulary but also in grammatical complexity (Hart & Risley, 1995, 1999).[1] It is not surprising that the lexicon and grammar stimulate and feed each other, since knowing a word means knowing how to use it in a sentence.

---

[1] We are aware of the current debates on this issue in the scholarly literature and in the general press. We are not commenting on parent behavior here but only making the connection between input and exposure, on the one hand, and richer vocabulary and grammar, on the other. This connection will be very important when we discuss second language speakers.

When learning new verbs and their grammatical shapes, children demonstrate the productive – in the sense of rule-based or predictable – nature of language development. After acquiring a number of past-tense forms of regular verbs such as *painted,* they discover a rule, namely, that past-tense forms are comprised of a root (*paint*) and an ending (*-ed*). Then, they generalize, applying the discovered rule to irregular verbs: instead of *held*, children might say *holded.* This is interesting because "holded" is not a form that children would have ever heard, since adults never use it. This inventive use of a grammar rule is adjusted when the correct irregular forms are finally learned, but it affords us a window into the language-learning process. Watch Steven Pinker, a prominent language researcher, talk about it in this video:www.youtube.com/watch?v=ir7arILiqxg.

Another illustration of the generative nature of human language is the story of Nicaraguan sign language. In the 1980s, a group of deaf children in Nicaragua created a new language because they had no common language to use. Scientists had never had the opportunity to witness and study such a process before. This newly created language exhibited all the hallmarks of a natural language, including those present in other sign languages. Conditions crucial for its creation were the high number of children brought together in Managua's first school for the deaf and the relative isolation of the community that guaranteed that no other sign language was available and known to the children. Linguists have identified many features that this new language has in common with other natural languages, thus substantiating linguist Noam Chomsky's idea that creating language is a natural biological process, just like learning to walk. You can read more about it and examine some pictures here: www.atlasobscura.com/articles/what-is-nicaraguan-sign-language.[2]

In summary, children acquire language rapidly and without much trial and error. Vocabulary development is closely related to grammar development; constraints on the mapping of form and meaning appear to work in both domains. In the next section, we will examine these constraints in greater depth.

1.4 Current Views of Language Acquisition

When deaf children create a new language, or when toddlers put together their first sentences, they are utilizing more than the signs and grammar they have seen or heard. At the core of the generative approach to language and language acquisition is the concept of Universal Grammar (UG), the common blueprint

---

[2] Watch these additional videos for more on this fascinating story.
  www.youtube.com/watch?v=pjtioIFuNf8,
  www.youtube.com/watch?v=U1I7IHY6xc4.

of all languages, or the genetically determined aspect of the human capacity for grammatical knowledge.

Over the years, this concept has undergone considerable theoretical reconsideration and is now one of three equally important components. Generative views of language acquisition are currently guided by Chomsky's (2005) *three factors* that determine the nature of language as an internally represented grammatical system:

F1: Genetic endowment (UG);
F2: Experience, or primary linguistic data (PLD); and
F3: Principles not specific to the language faculty.

The first factor is the species-specific UG – the grammatical knowledge by which all languages are constrained, and which is used in first and subsequent language acquisition. Notably, UG has been substantially reduced in size and complexity in current iterations of generative linguistic theory. The reader should not imagine UG as a localized neurological structure somewhere in the brain, or a device, or a tool. Instead, UG is an abstraction for the species-specific language knowledge.

The second factor is exposure to the linguistic input. Learners arrive at form–meaning connections by mapping signs to extralinguistic situations. Following Carroll (2017), we conceive of "input" as all the language that learners are potentially able to hear and read, while "exposure" is the observable and measurable input that a particular learner is exposed to. Language "experience" is a wider term and a relational notion; it is also determined by individual factors, including bilingualism, shared attention, social interaction, the amount and diversity of exposure to input, etc.

The third factor comprises general biological, physical, and computational laws of two kinds: first, principles of data analysis that are used in language acquisition but might also be part of other domains of cognition; and second, architectural constraints that facilitate efficient computation (Chomsky, 2005). The three factors bring together psycholinguistics and language acquisition: as learners parse their native language input, they acquire the grammatical features of that language (Lidz & Gagliardi, 2015). Acquisition happens unconsciously and simultaneously at all different levels of the grammar system: phonology, morphology, syntax, semantics, discourse, pragmatics.

1.5 What Is There to Learn in SLA?

Now let's consider the acquisition process from the second language perspective. If the mind generates language in predictable ways, does this predictability help people learn a second language? The short answer is, yes. As in child language acquisition, second language knowledge stems from the same three essential sources of information. In what follows, we will explore the notion that child language acquisition and adult second language acquisition are fundamentally similar processes.

The first source of information about the L2 is still Universal Grammar, the common blueprint of all languages. This blueprint includes information such as: all languages have nouns, verbs, prepositions, adjectives, and adverbs that express lexical meanings and combine with derivational and functional information; all languages have grammatical features (such as plural, case, definiteness, or genericity), whether these are expressed overtly or configured on lexical items or not; sentence meaning is compositionally read off word meanings taking their order into account; and discourse and context effects can change that sentential meaning.

From the birth of generative linguistics in the 1950s, generative linguists expressed the notion of UG via the "logical problem of language acquisition." The rationale went like this: language is complicated but children appear to acquire their first language relatively fast and without much trial and error. They must be doing this with some help from innate capacities. There must be facets of language knowledge that children do not need to discover for themselves because these facets constitute part of humans' biological endowment for language. This argument was naturally extended to SLA by researchers such as Lydia White (1985, 1989). Building an internalized grammatical system is at the core of both first and second language development, and discovering the nature of this fundamental process is key to understanding the whole edifice. More on evidence for UG in the next section.

Chomsky's (2005) second factor, naturalistic exposure to the new language, is equally crucial for SLA. Just as with children, the more diverse and varied and extensive the exposure, the easier it is to learn the new language. Just compare the exposure of two different hypothetical groups: the first, foreign language learners with a few hours of classroom tuition a week; the second, foreign language learners who are immersed in the country where the language is spoken natively. In terms of hours of daily exposure alone, the second type of learner has a pronounced advantage, which could lead to more effective acquisition (all other factors being equal). Finally, second language learners (known as 'L2ers') can certainly utilize the third-factor principles of computation not specific to language – an observation we will return to in the later sections. In this process, L2 learners utilize computation of structures from their native language but also gleaned from the input (Dekydtspotter & Renaud, 2014; Sharwood Smith, 2017).

However, there is an important difference between the L1 and L2 acquisition processes: second and subsequent language learners have already acquired one (or more) language(s). The native language appears to be a critical source of information, at least in the beginning. SLA scholars have convincingly shown that the native language provides the first hypothesis of how the new language works. Generative scholars (Schwartz & Sprouse, 1996; White, 1989) express this idea in the following way: The initial state of second language acquisition is the final state of first language acquisition. In other words, we approach the second language assuming that every property in it might work in the same way it does in our native language. Only when we have evidence to the contrary, provided by exposure to the second language, do we adjust the L1 assumption to something approximating the L2 property.

We come now to the central question of this section: What is there to learn in a second or additional language? The generative answer has changed over the years. When GenSLA came into being in the 1980s, the answer was formulated in terms very similar to those of principles and parameters (Chomsky, 1981). Principles constitute the universal information common to all languages that does not need to be learned and comes for free from UG. Parameters are options on what the UG "hypothesis space" offers as constraints on what is a possible natural grammar. The Null Subject Parameter and some word order parameters were the first to be investigated (White, 1985).

An intriguing idea popular at the time was the parametric cluster. To illustrate this concept, let's examine Snyder's (2001) Compounding Parameter. This parameter unifies several constructions in a cluster: productive noun–noun compounds, as in (1); the verb–particle construction, as in (2); the double object construction, as in (3); resultative predicates (4); and *make* causatives (5). The idea of a parametric cluster is that there is one underlying property in the grammar that, when acquired, activates all the (superficially unrelated) constructions of the cluster, so that they will be acquired simultaneously. In this case, the property underlying this cluster is the availability of so-called complex predicate constructions, which commonly involve the compounding of two roots, as exemplified in (1):

(1) *the car story* (possible meanings include the story about a/the car; a story about how the car was developed as a means of transportation; the story that someone told me in the car, as opposed to the one they told me on the train, etc.)

(2) *The children drank their cokes up.*

(3) *The children gave their mother a good scare.*

(4) *John wiped the counter clean.*

(5) *Mary made the children scream with excitement.*

Why were these constructions hypothesized to be in a parametric cluster? Because they occur together in languages around the world. Languages that do not allow root–root compounds productively, such as Spanish, do not have the rest of the constructions either. Yet the reality is more complex: languages that have verb particles, as in (2), do permit the free creation of root–root compounds, but not the other way around. In other words, there are several other conditions that have to fall into place for verb particles to be available in any given language. Snyder made the following acquisition prediction: a child learning English would either acquire compounding first, or acquire compounding and verb particles at the same time. In no case would a child acquire verb particles *before* compounding. This prediction was tested in the longitudinal development of twelve English-learning children, and it was strongly supported by this data (Snyder, 2001). It was also tested in second language acquisition (Slabakova, 2002). These findings did not contradict the clustering idea but, because the data was not longitudinal, the support for this parameter was not as strong.

During the time that the Principles and Parameters view of the grammar was dominant in linguistic theory and in GenSLA, the main research question was whether second language learners had access to UG. But how did researchers attempt to answer this question? Typically, by investigating properties that had different parametric values in the first and second languages. The logic was as follows: if researchers could find evidence that the second language parameter was acquired, this was considered support for the notion that learners had access to UG. This conclusion followed because the languages in question had different parametric values, such that knowledge of the L1 parameter would not help acquisition of the L2 parameter.

A pioneering study in this area was carried out by linguist Gita Martohardjono (1993), who tested learners' knowledge of long-distance English *wh*-questions. English questions, as we know, start with *wh*-words, like *where*, *what*, and *who*. Other languages, however, do not front these words, and so they may appear in their original positions in the declarative sentence. For this study, Martohardjono chose learners whose first language, unlike English, did not front *wh*-words (Indonesian and Chinese).[3] Thus, with respect to the *wh*-movement parameter, these languages exhibit values opposite to those in English. Martohardjono also took advantage of the fact that *wh*-movement violations have different degrees of severity. For instance, the example in (6), which is affectionately known by linguists as a violation

---

[3] Martohardjono also included Italian native speakers learning English; Italian works just like English with respect to *wh*-movement.

of the complex NP constraint with a moved object, feels ever so slightly less unacceptable than the one in (7), where the moved element is a subject instead. Linguists describe this distinction as a "weak" versus a "strong island" violation.

(6)   *Which movie did Mary hear a rumor that you had seen?*
(7)   **Who did Mary hear a rumor that had seen "Gone with the Wind"?*

Because both of these sentences are violations of some sort, they exemplify how speakers can be sensitive to subtle differences in acceptability.

So how do second language learners of English who speak Indonesian or Chinese acquire these distinctions – and do they, in fact, acquire them? To start with, differences in sensitivity to these violations cannot come from the input, because native speakers don't produce sentences such as these. Additionally, these distinctions cannot be learned in a classroom setting because teachers do not explain such ungrammatical constructions. This should not be surprising because native English speakers, unless they happen to be linguists, are not consciously aware of these distinctions in the first place. Finally, the distinction cannot come from the learners' native grammars, because these languages do not allow overt movement of the *wh*-phrase to the left periphery of the sentence. Martohardjono's results represented a major coup for the nascent GenSLA inquiry because she convincingly showed that advanced Indonesian and Chinese speakers made a significant distinction when evaluating sentences such as (6) and (7), mirroring the behavior of native speakers.

Another example was carried out by Kazue Kanno (1997), who studied pronouns in Japanese. Japanese, unlike English, includes in its inventory special pronouns aptly known as *null pronouns* because they are not pronounced. Languages that allow such pronouns are called Null-Subject languages and include typologically unrelated languages such as Chinese, Turkish, and Spanish. Interestingly, many languages in this family have a special restriction on how overt pronouns can be interpreted, known as the Overt Pronoun Constraint. This constraint does not allow for quantifiers such as *everyone* to corefer with overt pronouns. To better understand this restriction, let's examine examples (8) and (9). In each example, we have two pronouns in the beginning of the embedded clause surrounded by square brackets: the null pronoun (marked Ø) in (8) and *he* in (9). What the subindices [$_i$] mean is that in (8), the null pronoun and *who* can refer to the same person. In other words, the answer can be, for example, Roger said that Roger himself bought a car. This reading is impossible with the overt pronoun *kare* 'he' as in (9).

(8) *Dare_i ga   [Ø_i kuruma o katta to] itta no?*
Who NOM   car ACC bought that said Q
'Who_i said that (he_i) bought a car?'

(9) **Dare_i ga [kare_i ga kuruma o katta to]   itta no?*
who NOM he NOM car ACC bought that said Q
'Who_i said that he_i bought a car?'

In English, of course, sentence (8) is unacceptable with a null pronoun in the embedded clause (**Who said that bought a car?*), so the Overt Pronoun Constraint does not operate. What Kanno found was that, even though the Overt Pronoun Constraint is not obeyed in their first language, learners' judgments were like Japanese native speakers' judgments in that they allowed null pronouns to corefer with the *wh*-word while not allowing this coreference for *kare*.

In the 2000s, the prominence of Principles and Parameters in GenSLA research gave way to grammatical features with Lardiere's Feature Reassembly Hypothesis (Lardiere, 2009; Liceras, Zobl, & Goodluck, 2008, and articles therein). Formal features such as case, person, gender, and number are considered to be the building blocks of grammatical representations. Semantic features such as definiteness, specificity, uniqueness, past, and perfective are also proposed to be represented in functional categories. All these features in various combinations are expressed on lexical items such as verbs and nouns, and reflected in functional categories on a linguistic tree structure. For example, the verb *goes* in (10) expresses the features 3rd person, singular, present, and habitual action.

(10) *Lydia regularly go-**es** to yoga classes.*

In addition, the functional category Tense also captures the information that the subject *Lisa* is in nominative case and that the verb remains lower than the adverb *regularly* (thus in the Verb Phrase, VP) in English clause structure.

It is argued that L2 learning is better described and explained by investigating knowledge of feature meanings and expressions on lexical items, as well as the combinatorial restrictions of those features. The Feature Reassembly Hypothesis emphasizes that acquisition of a language's functional morphology involves much more than acquiring binary parametric values. Assembling the particular second language lexical items requires that learners reconfigure features from the way these are represented in the first language (Lardiere, 2009: 173). We will discuss this hypothesis in the following section.

Let's see an example of features via the Korean plural marker -*tul* (e.g. *chinkwu-tul 'friends'*). If plural marking were presented as a parameter,

Korean and English would have a plus value because plural is morphologic-ally marked and the morpheme means "more than two." Unlike in English, however, plural marking is optional in Korean (Kwon & Zribi-Hertz, 2004; Lardiere, 2009). Moreover, again unlike English, plural-marked nouns in Korean have to be specific in meaning, or known to speakers and hearers (Hwang & Lardiere, 2013; Kwon & Zribi-Hertz, 2004). Thus, even before we discuss co-occurrence with quantifiers and classifiers, there are marked dif-ferences in the expression of plural in Korean and English: optionality and specificity. Observations about linguistic differences of this magnitude prompted the reorientation to features as units of grammar that better reflect variation across languages.

1.6 Do We Get Any Help from Universal Grammar?

A major tenet of GenSLA is the existence of UG as part of a biologically endowed human language faculty. The postulation of UG is also the main distinction between GenSLA and other cognitive branches of SLA known as "usage-based approaches." Usage-based approaches embrace several different positions, but we will unify and simplify their message here. Usage-based views of language acquisition (Bybee, 2008; Ellis, 2002; Tomasello, 2003) posit that linguistic representations, both in the first and in the second language, are created without any help from innate capacities. Rather, the input is sufficient to model all language knowledge. The human brain can be likened to a powerful computer, which observes the regularities in the language a speaker is exposed to, and generalizes over these regularities to extract categories, phrase structure, and constructions.

GenSLA also assumes the process through which most linguistic mental representations are created is dependent on abundant exposure. Type, token, and collocation frequency are important in learning vocabulary as well as functional morphology. Even so, there are certain properties that allow us glimpses into the functioning of UG. For generative scholars, the cases that suggest an operation of an innate language acquisition device and make all the difference are those described as Poverty-of-the-Stimulus (PoS) situations. These are properties of language that cannot be acquired solely based on the input – they require some form of negative evidence. Often, these properties come in the shape of negative constraints: a structure that analogy suggests should be allowed by the grammar but it is not allowed, or a meaning that should be possible to compute but it is not. Since these negative constraints cannot be exemplified with positive evidence, it is contended that successful acquisition is based on some innate part of the grammar.

We already saw an example of this in the weak versus strong island constraints in Martohardjono's work. There is a subtle difference in acceptability in two English unacceptable constructions that learners never hear, but they are still sensitive to this difference. For even more examples, we refer readers to a recent review of such properties by Schwartz and Sprouse (2013), which elaborates on five different types of PoS properties. An important point to keep in mind is that the existence of PoS learning situations is no longer a theoretical necessity but a matter of observation and ultimately of empirical evidence. Every PoS case must be defined, defended, and tested on its own (Rothman & Slabakova, 2018). We must also keep in mind that a great deal of language information comes from the mother tongue, not necessarily directly from UG.

1.7 Conclusion

In this section, we introduced key concepts in GenSLA that inform our current understanding of what language is and how humans acquire it. We identified Universal Grammar as one factor of language design, the other two being linguistic experience and general computation principles. We argued that these three factors are also vital in second language acquisition, with the important addition of the native language as another factor. We saw that while principles and parameters were the main objects of early GenSLA inquiry in GenSLA, attention has shifted to features as building blocks of grammatical knowledge. Poverty-of-the-Stimulus learning situations, as far as they stand scrutiny, suggest that UG remains a source of second language knowledge, together with the native language and knowledge obtained through L2 exposure and use.

2 What Are the Main Branches of Research?

2.1 Current GenSLA Theories and Research Branches

We introduced some key concepts that GenSLA researchers hold about the architecture of language and about what we acquire when learning a second language. Building on that knowledge, we turn to research branches within generative research that tell us about the factors that matter in second language acquisition and propose theories that attempt to explain it. Here, we explore a select number of research branches, including research that attempts to explain what is difficult and what is easy to learn in a second language (or, more drastically: what we must learn and what comes for free). Importantly, these branches of research also attempt to explain *why* this is the case.

2.2 Two Vital Research Branches in Generative SLA: Investigating L1 Influence and Access to Universal Grammar

When generative researchers ponder questions such as, 'What is easy and what is hard when learning a second language?', or when they investigate the reasons behind this inquiry, many focus on two specific issues. The first is the role played by the first language in the acquisition of the second (the question of language transfer, which we shall define). This question makes intuitive sense because the first language has been shown to be an important factor in second language acquisition. Generative researchers assume the existence of a genetically determined blueprint for learning language, a Universal Grammar (UG). Because of this assumption, a second essential question relates to whether second language learners have access to this capacity after the first language has been acquired.

Let us first consider the question of the influence of the first language on the second, or *first language (L1) transfer*. The generative study of L2 acquisition is well suited to address this question because generative linguistics has focused on modeling the nature of mental representations. Using constructs such as 'parameters' or 'features', linguists have endeavored to delineate how the second language is acquired and represented in speakers' minds. Thus, within generative research, we can determine *what* transfers from the first language because detailed descriptions exist for myriad structures in many languages, which we can use to determine L1 transfer.

Intuitively, we can say that one of the most evident differences between the acquisition of a first and a second language is prior experience: when we begin to learn a second language, we don't do so with a blank slate because we already speak a language – our mother tongue. This means we not only have lexical items to describe the world around us, but also detailed abstract language representations – a *generative grammar* – that allow us to put an infinite number of sentences together in real time. The question, then, is an empirical one: What is the starting point when learning a second language? For generative linguists, this has typically been posited as a question of transfer.

If we entertain logical possibilities, we could posit at least three scenarios regarding transfer. The first is that when we learn a second language, our initial hypotheses are guided by our native grammar – in other words, that we have *Full Transfer* of our L1 abstract linguistic system. The researchers Bonnie Schwartz and Rex Sprouse have proposed such a learning situation (Schwartz & Sprouse, 1996), arguing that the initial state of the L2 acquisition process is the L1 abstract system. A second logical possibility is that some, but not all, of the properties of our native language transfer into our second. In other words, learners depart from an incomplete set of properties, or what is known as *Partial Transfer*. Researchers such as the late Anne Vainikka and Martha Young-Sholten (Vainikka & Young-Sholten, 1994) have endorsed such a proposal. The third and (so far) final possibility is that there is *No Transfer* of the native language's properties into the second (Epstein, Flynn, & Martohardjono, 1996).

It is worth stressing at this point that when researchers adjudicate between competing theories such as the previous three regarding transfer, they weigh the evidence that can falsify a theory or hypothesis. In this particular case, what can we take as evidence to determine which of these proposals is on the right track? Because we are talking about the initial state of L2 acquisition, we concentrate on beginning learners and, following linguist Lydia White (White, 1989, 2003), we would look for evidence of L1 properties in the emerging L2 grammar (typically referred to as *interlanguage*).

Consider now the case of a Turkish child learning English. This combination of languages is relevant because Turkish and English behave differently when it comes to the ordering of the words in a sentence. While English is an SVO (subject-verb-object) language, Turkish is a verb-final language. Thus, if we anticipate L1 transfer of linguistic properties, we would predict that the utterances of this beginning English L2 learner would show the verb-final influence of Turkish. In fact, this is exactly what the researcher Belma Haznedar (Haznedar, 1997) investigated. She studied a four-year-old child whose native language was Turkish and analyzed the child's spontaneous production of English after the child was first introduced to the language. Evidence for L1 transfer comes from the child producing English utterances such as *I something eating* (a verb-final utterance that would be grammatical in Turkish), which the child produced before producing more English-like forms such as *I not eat cornflake*.

Beyond this case study, we also have experimental evidence from researchers such as Roumyana Slabakova (Slabakova, 2000), who studied the acquisition of English by a group of adult learners whose L1 was either Spanish or Bulgarian. Slabakova studied the acquisition of properties within the verb phrase (telicity, more specifically) because Spanish and Bulgarian sit at opposite ends of the telicity spectrum, with Spanish but not Bulgarian following a pattern much like that in English. Neither English nor Spanish mark telicity on the verb, instead marking it through the object of the sentence. Specifically, events denoted as 'Telic' are associated with objects that can be measured or counted (e.g. 'three cakes'/*tres pasteles* [Sp]), while 'atelic' events lack that specification (e.g. 'cakes'/*pasteles* [Sp])). Bulgarian, on the other hand, marks telicity via morphological markings on the verb. Thus, if we are searching for evidence of L1 transfer with these language combinations, we would expect to find *positive transfer* effects (convergence with the native forms) in the Spanish group and *negative transfer* effects (lack of convergence with the native forms) in the Bulgarian group. While we won't attempt a detailed review of the findings, this is exactly what Slabakova found. Given the English/Spanish similarities in telicity marking, beginning Spanish learners were accurate when interpreting (a)telicity in English, while Bulgarian speakers only converged on those forms that they could directly trace to their L1. While there is much more research in this area, suffice it to say that Full-Transfer hypotheses have received a good deal of support from empirical investigations and remain one of the most influential in generative SLA studies.

We began by touching on two essential inquiries: L1 transfer and access to universal principles. After our brief exploration of L1 transfer, we can now move on to the second question, which involves access to the biological endowment that is our capacity for grammatical knowledge: Universal Grammar. As before, let's consider some logical possibilities. The first possibility, known as *Full Access* to UG, proposes that second language learners have access to UG, meaning the development of their second language can be guided – and restructured – by universal principles (Schwartz & Sprouse, 1996). If we assume UG is operative in L1 acquisition, as we suggested previously, a second logical possibility is that learners have access to UG in a limited way – for instance, via the universal properties that are *already* instantiated in our native tongue, a possibility known as *Partial Access*. We will discuss here a subset of Partial-Access hypotheses collectively known as the *Representational Deficit Hypotheses*, proposed by linguists such as Ianthi Tsimpli, Roger Hawkins, and their associates (e.g. Hawkins & Casillas, 2008; Hawkins & Chan, 1997; Tsimpli & Dimitrakopoulou, 2007).

Earlier, we mentioned that Schwartz and Sprouse proposed full transfer of L1 properties, but now we are in a position to review their full proposal: Schwartz and Schwartz propose that, while the initial state is the L1 grammar, learners are not preordained to keep the L1 values forever (a situation known by some as *fossilization* or, perhaps less negatively, *stabilization*). Instead, they propose that learners' L2 grammar, their interlanguage, can be restructured such that L1 values can match the L2 values, at least in principle. Their proposal, aptly termed the *Full Transfer/Full Access Hypothesis*, is thus a representational theory that accounts for both the L2 initial state as well as the subsequent development of the L2 grammar.

At the other end of the spectrum, Representational Deficit Hypotheses (RDH) share with Full Transfer/Full Access the assumption that the L1 is transferred. The crucial difference is that RDH proposals suggest that Access to UG is, in a sense, impaired in second language acquisition, such that a subset of linguistic features known as "uninterpretable features" are inaccessible unless they can be transferred from the first language. At this point, we must stop and ask: what are uninterpretable features, exactly?

The distinction between interpretable and uninterpretable features goes back again to Chomsky (Chomsky, 1995, 2001). In short, a *feature* is a linguistic element that carries meaning. Chomsky noted that this meaning can be either conceptual (in other words, the feature contributes to the meaning of a word, or what we call *semantic interpretation*) or grammatical (i.e. functional in the sense that it performs a function within the grammar). Under this view, *interpretable features* carry conceptual meanings that can be interpreted by our Conceptual-Intentional system. Uninterpretable features, however, do not contribute to the semantic meaning but can, instead, indicate a grammatical function such as whether a given phrase is a subject or an object (typically known as the *case* marking of a phrase), or whether it indicates grammatical gender, among other functional meanings.

Representational Deficit Hypotheses (RDH) build on the interpretability distinction and propose that uninterpretable features cannot be acquired by L2 learners. The practical implication is that learners' abstract representations of the second language are handicapped, in a sense, because, by hypothesis, learners do not have access to UG beyond those properties represented in their L1. This proposal is also crucially linked to another important construct, namely, the possibility of a *Critical Period* in second language acquisition (Lenneberg, 1967). Briefly summarized, the Critical Period Hypothesis proposes that the acquisition of a second language is more difficult, perhaps impossible, after the onset of puberty. Specifically, the Critical Period Hypothesis suggests that although learners can acquire new lexical vocabulary, they might not reach mastery of all L2 grammatical structures (Slabakova, 2016).[4]

Given this state of affairs, what would constitute evidence for or against Full Transfer/Full Access vs. RDH? Let's take a classic case of acquisitional difficulty: acquiring grammatical gender by adult L1 speakers of a (grammatically) genderless language (such as English). According to RDH, because English lacks grammatical gender, English speakers will face inordinate difficulties when acquiring a grammatically gendered language such as Spanish. Although English and Spanish instantiate biological gender (e.g. words like

---

[4] An anonymous reviewer rightly points out that our discussion of the Critical Period Hypothesis is rather short, since it is not the main aim of the section nor the Element. As such, we do not dwell on important terminological differences such as that between "critical" and "sensitive" periods. Interested readers are referred to work by Birdsong (1999) and Granena and Long (2013), among many others, for details.

woman vs. *man* encode biological gender differences), only Spanish encodes *grammatical gender*. Nouns in Spanish are either masculine (*el ascensor* 'the elevator') or feminine (*la lámpara* 'the lamp'). Crucially, Spanish determiners (e.g. articles such as the equivalents of "a," "an," or "the") and adjectives (e.g. *bello/bella* 'beautiful') agree with or 'match' the grammatical gender of the noun. Because this agreement is triggered by uninterpretable features, success in the acquisition of gender represents support for Full Transfer/Full Access, while failure constitutes support for RDH.

Although we know quite a bit about gender acquisition, in this regard, the proverbial jury is still out. Some investigations have found that L1 speakers of languages that lack grammatical gender experience great difficulty with gender agreement when they learn languages such as French or Spanish, even when they have reached high levels of mastery. Other investigations, however, have established that learners can represent and process gender in a native-like manner even if their first language lacks grammatical gender (e.g. Sagarra & Herschensohn, 2013; White et al., 2004).

We have seen that generative SLA researchers have keenly investigated L1 transfer and access to UG in second language acquisition. While these conversations, especially those regarding access to UG, are still ongoing, generative researchers have also proposed other theories, to which we turn next.

2.3 Research Branches Focusing on Acquiring Functional Morphology

While the questions of transfer and access dominated generative SLA studies through the late nineties, many researchers also turned their attention to a linguistic domain that appeared, at times, to pose an insurmountable challenge for second language learners: the acquisition of functional morphology. When faced with such an unbending problem, a logical question to ponder is: Why is morphology so hard to acquire? In this section, we will review proposals that attempt to explain this puzzle.

Before proceeding, let's address the question of what functional morphology is and does. Within modern generative linguistics, morphology is a special linguistic domain because it hosts the differences between the world's languages. Even reduced to its most basic definition, functional morphology is complex and multifaceted because it pairs *a form* (a sound or written form) with *a grammatical meaning* but also, crucially, it is of importance to the syntax, often regulating which parts of the sentences get to move around and which remain in their original position. The practical consequence of the different functions that morphology performs is that morphological rules guide a great variety of grammatical functions, including how to build words that are complex (how to derive *frogs* from *frog* and *foxes* from *fox* but also *worked* from *work* and *sang* from *sing*) or to determine which words can appear in a given linear order (compare *"You will not look as nice when you are 50 years old"* with the more Yoda-like *"When 900 years old you reach look as good you will not"*).

Generative linguists have accounted for difficulty with the acquisition of morphology in multiple ways. To survey some of these accounts, we return to our old friend, the linguistic feature.

2.3.1 One Explanation: The Feature Reassembly Hypothesis

When acquiring a second language, we must acquire its morphological features in all their beautiful complexity: the sound/form, the grammatical meaning, and its import to syntax. The problem is that when we learn a second language, we *already* have a template of how these features work – albeit in our first language. Because there is ample evidence that we transfer our abstract knowledge of the L1 when we are learning our L2, this transfer can cause considerable problems when the languages in question differ. This is exactly what the linguist Donna Lardiere was concerned with when she proposed the Feature Reassembly Hypothesis (Lardiere, 2009).

Let us consider a young adult whose first language is English and is now learning French and having a terrible time learning direct object pronouns. English and French both have pronouns for direct objects, but these function in different ways when it comes to expressing the linguistic feature [human]. On the one hand, English encodes this feature [human] in its pronoun inventory, such that *him* and *her* refer to [+human] entities, while *it* encodes the opposite, [–human]. This picture is complicated by the fact that English only encodes *biological gender* with humans and not with nonhuman entities. French direct object pronouns, on the other hand, hold less regard for the [human] feature and focus on grammatical gender instead: the pronoun *le* can be used with [+human] AND [–human] entities as long as these are masculine (analogously, *la* can be used with [+human] and [–human] entities which are feminine). Faced with these differences, what is a learner to do?

To determine how second language learners go about acquiring these pesky pronouns, linguist Elena Shimanskaya set out to examine these featural mismatches following Lardiere's proposal that restructuring features (or "reassembly" of features, as she has it) can be problematic in second language acquisition (Shimanskaya, 2015). If we assume, following Lardiere's Feature Reassembly Hypothesis, that there is L1 transfer, we can immediately see we have a mismatch: English-speaking learners of French must realize that there are only two direct object pronoun forms (*la* and *le*) rather than three (*him*, *her* and *it*) and, moreover, that these do not encode [human] status but grammatical (not biological) gender – obviously a difficult task! Shimanskaya used a task where learners selected pictures that could co-refer to pronouns to determine whether they would correctly match, for instance, the pronoun *la* with *both* human and nonhuman referents (e.g. *Anne* and *la table* [Fr, feminine]) as long as the grammatical gender of the referents matched that of the pronoun (feminine, in this case).

Shimanskaya's results point to interesting conclusions. Because she tested learners at different levels of proficiency, she could determine the presence of L1 transfer. As expected, learners at the lower end of the proficiency spectrum showed more difficulty with [–human] referents (which display grammatical gender in French) because these did not match their English-style feature bundles. On the other hand, novice learners were more accurate with [+human] referents because these are marked for biological gender in English and thus learners enjoyed the benefits of positive transfer. Beyond transfer, however, these results also show that while feature reassembly is arduous, it is possible. The evidence comes from the behavior of more advanced learners, who were able to perform in a native-like fashion. These findings suggest that if learners can find enough evidence in the input, they can restructure their L1 English grammar and successfully learn French object pronouns in this particular case. As we will see shortly, however, this is far from an easy task because getting access to the linguistic input that would trigger this change may not always be possible.

2.3.2 A Second Explanation: Morphology as the Bottleneck of Acquisition

By now, we know that the acquisition of functional morphology is quite complex and that it is related to syntax. A natural question to ask, then, is: Can we separate syntax from morphology? If the answer is negative, it might be the case that the complexity of morphology stems from its relationship to syntax.

Roumyana Slabakova (Slabakova, 2016) set out to answer this question and noted that we have independent evidence from acquisition studies that learning complex syntactic restrictions and rules, while difficult, is not impossible – if and when the associated functional morphology is acquired. This is not a small caveat. Slabakova also uncovered evidence that the acquisition of semantic and pragmatic structures can proceed smoothly when and if the necessary functional morphology has been acquired. Based, in part, on these collective findings, Slabakova proposed the *Bottleneck Hypothesis*.

Slabakova's logical argument proceeds thus: First, she departs from the notion that functional morphology is a complex pairing of sound/grammatical meanings and that functional morphology also functions as a repository of grammatical meanings and functions that represent the differences between languages. In the absence of (functional) morphological knowledge, speakers could not comprehend language and would have a hard time analyzing word strings beyond the most basic meanings (for instance, based on semantically rich vocabulary items). Assuming the existence of syntactic and semantic universal principles, a clearer picture emerges: *the site of difficulty is the site of difference – functional morphology*. Based on evidence that complex syntactic properties and semantic calculations can be acquired only when the proper functional morphology is learned, Slabakova assumes that morphology functions as a bottleneck, creating a "tight place" complicating acquisition.

Because the Bottleneck Hypothesis is a "young" proposal, there is room for investigation, but it already enjoys empirical support. A study by Jensen and colleagues (Jensen et al., 2020) focused on native speakers of Norwegian learning English and investigated the learners' knowledge of functional morphology and of syntax. Norwegian, like many Germanic languages, has special verb-placement restrictions within main clauses – a restriction that earns these languages the moniker of "V2 languages." At the risk of oversimplifying, V2 languages restrict the placement of finite (roughly, "conjugated") verbs to the second position in a main clause, following a constituent that is considered the main clause's "topic."

Armed with this bit of knowledge, we can predict that Norwegian native speakers can encounter potential difficulties in the acquisition of English syntax because English is an SVO language, where verb-placement restrictions are related to a syntactic function (subject precedes verb) rather than a linear order (topic first, verb second). Thus, a sentence like "*Yesterday went the teacher to the shop" is not grammatical in English, although its Norwegian analogue would be. In addition to testing sentences such as this, the authors also tested subject-verb agreement, which is obligatory in English but not in Norwegian, in order to determine whether morphology created the "tight spot" predicted by the Bottleneck Hypothesis. In fact, this is exactly what these researchers found: learners were tested on their knowledge of syntax (the lack of V2 effects in English) and morphology (obligatory subject-verb agreement in English) and they performed as predicted by the Bottleneck Hypothesis. Namely, they were successful in rejecting sentences such as *Yesterday went the teacher to the shop* while accepting ungrammatical sentences such as *The brown dog play with the yellow football*, which failed to display subject–verb agreement in English.

While there is much more to say and more proposals to review on the acquisition of morphology, we limit ourselves to the previous two for space reasons. So far, we have talked about L1 transfer, access to universal principles, and the intricacies of the acquisition of functional morphology. In what follows, we will review one recent area of investigation that identifies yet another site of difficulty in second language acquisition: linguistic interfaces.

2.4 Another Research Branch: Studying the Problem with Interfaces

Communicating with others involves actively coding and decoding linguistic messages uttered and perceived by speakers and hearers. As if by magic, this process unfolds in real time and, in our first language at least, seemingly without effort and within the span of milliseconds. When a word string is uttered, speakers produce acoustic waves composed by linguistic sounds that must be arranged according to the grammar of a given language. Within linguistics, the study of sounds and sound systems (the relationships among sounds) fall under the study of phonetics and phonology, respectively. Moreover, as we have already seen, when (de)coding linguistic messages, speakers follow the rules of syntax, morphology, and pragmatics. Finally, messages must be conceptually interpreted via a series of computational operations that follow the rules of semantics. Yet this is not all: beyond these linguistic domains, communication is contingent on extra-linguistic content because language happens in real-life situations, not in a vacuum. This state of affairs is true whether we speak a first or a second language. *Two natural questions to ask at this junction are:* How are these linguistic and extra-linguistic elements organized to achieve communication? and How do we keep track of the grammar and real-world content?

Within generative linguistics, linguistic domains such as syntax or semantics are posited to be separate but organized in a way that is *internal* to our abstract grammar. When a particular linguistic construction involves domains such as morphology and syntax, or syntax and semantics, we say that the construction involves an *internal interface*. On the other hand, the discourse context – the message's extra-linguistic content – is proposed to sit outside our abstract grammar; therefore, when discourse context interfaces with other grammatical modules (e.g. syntax), we speak of an *external interface*.

Linguist Antonella Sorace capitalized on this distinction in the *Interface Hypothesis* (Sorace, 2011). In essence, Sorace argues that keeping track of the discourse context and the grammar is not an easy task, especially when speakers have to do it under pressure (for instance, in live communication). In Sorace's estimation, this is particularly true for bilinguals because incorporating different types of information comes at a high cognitive cost. Thus, even if second language learners are able to restructure their grammar, the Interface Hypothesis predicts that learners might show variable application of rules and values, depending on the number of elements speakers have to keep track of.

Let's imagine an English speaker who is learning Italian, focusing on an area where English and Italian differ: subject expression. In English, overt subjects are required in every sentence, so sentences like *Ate cake or *Rained yesterday* cannot be interpreted. In Italian, however, an overt subject is not needed, so a sentence like *Ho mangiato la torta ieri* (literally: *Have eaten the cake yesterday*) is not only perfectly acceptable but often the most natural choice. Abstracting from some particulars, languages that can optionally pronounce subjects (languages that have both phonetically null *and* phonetically overt subjects) are called Null-Subject Languages. Italian, Spanish, and Turkish, to name a few, belong to this category. Languages like English, French, and German, however, are called Non-Null-Subject languages because phonetically null subjects are not possible.

Languages like Italian tend to have other characteristics that result from the possibility of having phonetically null subjects. One such characteristic is the availability of subjects called postverbal (they follow the verb). Thus, "*Arrived John" is not a grammatical sentence in English, but *E'arrivato Gianni* (literally: *Is arrived Gianni*) is perfectly fine in Italian. Yet another characteristic of null-subject languages relates to how pronouns are interpreted. To illustrate, let's analyze some Italian sentences (Belletti, Bennati, & Sorace, 2007).

1.   Maria$_i$ telefonerà   quando   **pro**$_{i/*j}$ ne avrà voglia.
     Maria will-call   when   null-pronoun   will feel like
     "Maria will call when she feels like it."

2.   Maria$_i$ telefonerà quando   **lei** $_{*i/j}$ ne avrà voglia.
     Maria will-call when   she   will feel like
     "Maria will call when she feels like it."

These sentences are in typical linguistic notation and indicate the null pronominal with the word "pro" (affectionately called '*little pro*'). In these examples, the subject of the clause (Maria) is indicated by the sub-index "i," following linguistic convention. Note that the null pronominal in sentence (1) also displays the sub-index "i," which indicates that little *pro* refers to the clause's subject (Maria). Note that the sub-index "j" is preceded by an asterisk (*), which means that this null pronominal is not interpreted as an external referent (someone else in the discourse). However, as sentence (2) indicates, an overt subject pronoun – *lei,* in this case – preferably refers to an external entity (as long as the referent is human and feminine). English, as a dutiful non-null-subject language, cannot offer these possibilities because, as shown by the translations, the pronoun is always present.

Let's return to the Interface Hypothesis. Because the interpretation of null and overt pronouns relies on the discourse (the person in the real world about whom we are talking), the expectation is that learners will struggle with this. Adriana Belletti and colleagues (Belletti, Bennati, & Sorace, 2007) investigated this question and found that native speakers of English who were near-native speakers of Italian did struggle to systematically map overt pronouns to external referents – exactly as predicted by the Interface Hypothesis. Because these learners also displayed knowledge on the syntactic restrictions of postverbal subjects, the authors argued that integrating syntax and discourse, rather acquiring syntax alone, was behind the variability in interpretations.

While the research emerging from this area shows that not all properties at the external interface are problematic, the evidence that there is something special about the integration of linguistic and extra-linguistic modules continues to draw the attention of researchers.

2.5 Main Branches of Research: Interim Conclusions

Clearly, the generative study of second language acquisition has advanced our understanding of the important factors underlying second language acquisition including L1 transfer, the reasons behind the difficulty in the acquisition of morphology, whether learners have access to universal principles that constrain grammatical representations, and even why they struggle to track referents in real-time discourse. While our review is short and, necessarily, incomplete, we hope to have shown how generative researchers think about the question of language acquisition and how the scientific method (observation/description, hypothesis creation and testing, modification, etc.) informs our inquiry.

While we endorse the plurality of theories and hypotheses in second language acquisition studies, we also hope to have shown the advantages of having a clearly articulated theory of language, which we can use to predict the areas of difficulty. In the next section, we will talk about an important implication for SLA that is related to the second factor in Chomsky's theorizing about language design: linguistic input.

3 What Are the Implications for SLA?

3.1 A Crucial Implication for SLA: The Importance of Input

Although there exist numerous implications that can be drawn from the generative study of second language acquisition, we will focus here on the importance of input. To start, let's return to Chomsky's (2005) seminal article "Three Factors in Language Design," which offers a recapitulation of generative thinking in the early twenty-first century. Chomsky lists the crucial components of language design – factors implicated not just in the evolution of human language, but also in the development of the language capacity in each individual. As introduced in Section 1, the first factor (F1) is the genetic endowment for language (UG) while the third (F3) comprises general principles of computation and cognition. The second factor (F2), and the topic of this section, is identified as "[e]xperience, which leads to variation within a fairly narrow range, as in the case of other subsystems of the human capacity and the organism generally" (Chomsky, 2005: 6). Chomsky proposes that F2 is not only the locus of linguistic diversity, but actually provides the trigger experience for acquisition, which proceeds through exposure to the primary linguistic data (PLD) (Chomsky, 2013: 37). Here, we first provide the current theoretical thinking on the role of the linguistic input in language acquisition. Then we examine GenSLA studies testing input effects in knowledge of morphosyntax. We conclude by pointing to the limits of experience, or what input cannot provide for second language learners.

3.2 Emergent Parameters

Let's first review a proposal of how variation among languages can be learned, put forth by a group of like-minded linguists including Ian Roberts, Anders Holmberg, Theresa Biberauer, Michelle Sheehan, and others (e.g. Holmberg & Roberts 2014). These researchers propose that knowledge about how languages differ (known as knowledge about parameters) "emerges" as an interaction of the three language-design factors. We say that their view of UG is *minimalist* because they assume that there are small parts of UG that are *underspecified*, and that the interaction between PLD and "the inherent computational conservatism of the learner" restricts the space of how languages can differ (Holmberg & Roberts, 2014: 63). Under this view, linguistic input (F2) represents the *triggering experience* that is indispensable for this emergent knowledge.

As an example, let's examine the passive construction (Holmberg & Roberts, 2014: 66), starting with the following examples:

(1) a. *The tiger was seen by everybody.*
     b. *Everybody saw the tiger.*
     c. *Es   wurde   gesungen   und   getanzt.*   [German]
         it   was   sung   and   danced
         'There was singing and dancing.'
     d. *The customer was paid $500 as compensation.*
     e. *$500 was paid to the customer as compensation.*

f. *Se*   *vendieron*   *los pisos*   (**por los propietarios*).   [Spanish]
   se$_{PASS}$ sold   the apartments   by the owners
   'The apartments were sold by the owners.'

Syntactically, we say that the passive structure in (1a) results from the object, the "Patient" argument in (1b), moving to subject position. This movement, known as "A-movement," is related to F1 because its constraints are set by UG. Passive constructions, however, exhibit additional variation in different languages: some languages, such as German, allow *impersonal passives* (1c); languages like English allow passives of ditransitive verbs[5] (1d, 1e); while others do not allow the *by*-phrase (e.g. Romance *se*-passives, 1f).

If languages differ in all these ways, how do humans go about learning them? If English speakers transfer their knowledge of the passive to their L2 German, the impersonal passive will not make part of the L2 grammar. Purportedly, these distinctions are learned through exposure to PLD, aided by UG. Passive constructions involve the thematic roles Agent and Patient,[6] which exchange grammatical function in passive constructions. These roles also involve aspects of the world, including events, causes, and intentions that pertain to general cognition. Thus, although learners who know the passive construction in any language can certainly be aided by F1 and F3, their exposure to enough PLD (F2) is crucial for them to fix the language-specific variation. Since F2 entails frequency, the next section focuses on frequency effects.

3.3 Frequency Effects on Parameter Evidence

The importance of linguistic input has been recognized from the beginning of the generative linguistics enterprise (Chomsky, 1957). However, the study of the properties of the input itself and the quantification of its effects had not garnered sufficient attention – until recently. This change was partially stimulated by the availability of sizeable child language corpora and child-directed speech data, which allowed the study of the properties of the input with increased focus. As we mentioned earlier, children's use of language is productive and rule-based; that is, they produce sentences they have never heard before. Children also produce errors that can only be classified as developmental, such as overgeneralization of past tense marking. It turns out that this behavior is also input-based.

---

[5] Roughly speaking, ditransitive verbs take three arguments, typically a subject and two objects. For instance, the verb *give* requires a subject, a direct object, and an indirect object. In the sentence *I gave Sebastian the tarantula*, all three arguments ([I], [Sebastian], [the tarantula]) are required.

[6] In a nutshell, we say that thematic roles are those that a noun phrase plays with respect to the actions (or states) described by a verb. In the sentence *Sienna petted the bunny*, the noun phrase *Sienna* is assigned the role of Agent, while the noun phrase *the bunny* plays a Patient role.

Charles Yang (Yang, 2002, 2004) has proposed that the input may provide more than just triggering experience. Yang studied children's grammars to determine how parameters were set, and in the process he convincingly demonstrated the existence of a relationship between parameter setting and frequency (Yang, 2012). Specifically, parameter values that children encounter more frequently are, those that they fix very early and without much deviation from the target. Examples of these are the fronting of question words (*wh*-words) in English, as well as Topic drop in Mandarin Chinese. On the other hand, parameter values for which there is scant evidence in the input, such as scope marking in English, are set relatively late, after the age of four.

It is interesting to consider what Yang assumes is the evidence for parameter setting. In his view, this evidence must be constituted either by a salient piece of morphology (Lightfoot, 1991) or by a related construction that unambiguously points to the parameter value. To explain what this means, let us take the property of verb second. As we mentioned in Section 2, a number of Germanic languages require that the verb be the second constituent in the sentence structure. This property is dubbed "V2."[7]

(2) a. *John kysset Mary.*   [Norwegian]
         John kissed Mary
     b. *John kissed Mary.*
     c. *I går   kysset John Mary.*   [Norwegian]
         yesterday   kissed John Mary
     d. *Yesterday John kissed Mary.*

Regular sentences with SVO word order (2a, b) do not provide irrefutable evidence that English does not instantiate "V2" (what we call the "minus" value of this parameter), meaning learners cannot use these types of sentences to set a V2 value. Only when sentences start with a non-subject constituent, such as with an adverbial like *yesterday,* can learners clearly see the parameter setting. The English verb *kissed* can be in third position, as (2d) shows, while the Norwegian sentence must have the verb in second position, as in (2c).

In this case, the question 'Is it UG? or is it statistical learning?' receives the answer, 'It is both.' We should note, however, that while there is ample evidence that this is the case in child language, hard evidence in second language acquisition is still largely missing (see Yang, 2018, for proposals).

---

[7] The V2 property, argued by some to be a parameter (e.g., Vikner, 1995), is more complex than we show here. Some authors argue that it is an assembly of several parameters (Weerman, 1989), at least in some languages such as Norwegian (Westergaard & Vangsnes, 2005).

3.4 What Does Input Give the Learner?

Another question related to the implications of input for SLA is: What is learnable, and what must be learned, from the input? For the sake of exposition, let's ponder two types of information, which we will present as separate although they always work in tandem.

Parameter values are one type of linguistic knowledge that, crucially, depends on unconscious observation and exposure to the input in sufficient quantity and quality. As an example, let's explore the acquisition of questions, the so-called *wh*-movement parameter in Bulgarian–English interlanguage. When learning this parameter, a learner must acquire that all *wh*-words in Bulgarian multiple *wh*-questions move to the left periphery of the sentence, as in (3). This is unlike what happens in English, as the translation on the third line of the example shows.

(3) *Koj   kogo   koga   celuna?*   [Bulgarian]
    Who   whom   when   kissed
    'Who kissed whom when?'

In addition to parameter-based acquisition, there is a large amount of information that is language-specific. Language-specific information constitutes perhaps the bulk of language learning and can be learned solely from the input. Foremost among this language-specific information is the acquisition of vocabulary (lexicon) with all its facets, which include phonetic, phonological, and morphological information. Again, it is important to note that this learning is inductive and data-driven (F3). For instance, a second language learner of Bulgarian must remember that the semantic equivalent of *cat* [kæt] is [kotka]. In addition, the learner has to acquire grammatical information such as the fact that *kotka* is feminine and agrees in gender and number with adjectives and participles. Because Bulgarian nouns are obligatorily gender-marked, learning the Bulgarian lexicon can be a challenge.

Let's take another example that nicely illustrates parametric versus lexicon-based learning. We mentioned it earlier, but we will expand its description here. In Bulgarian, telicity, or the meaning that indicates that the verbal action has a potential endpoint, is marked on the verb with a prefix, see (4a,b). In English, that same meaning is expressed through a dynamic verb and an object, see (5a,b).

(4) a. *Ivan **pro**-čete*   *knigata.*   (telic event)   [Bulgarian]
         Ivan PREF-read.PAST   book.DET
         'Ivan read the book.'

    b. *Ivan čete*   *knigata.*   (atelic event)
         Ivan read.PAST   book.DET
         'Ivan did some reading from the book/Ivan was reading the book.'

(5) a. Mary built **a house**.   (telic event)
    b. Sally built **houses** for a living.   (atelic event)

One could describe this linguistic distinction by saying it constitutes a parameter: a parameter of Aspect. Acquiring this broader difference is not difficult, since it is clearly expressed in the input. However, that is only part of the knowledge that needs to be acquired by learners of Bulgarian. The language has nineteen different prefix morphemes like the one in (4a), and they are lexically selected by different verbs (***pro-četa*** 'read to completion' but ***iz-yam*** 'eat up'). On top of telicity, these prefixes have additional meanings such as, 'Do all over again,' 'Do exhaustively,' and so on. The lexical challenge of learning the telicity markers is much more extensive than simply learning that telicity is marked with a prefix. Slabakova (2005) tested this distinction in Russian, a Slavic language presenting the same challenge as Bulgarian, and showed that it was the lexical learning that constituted the most substantial challenge for the learners. This is analogous to what we discussed in Section 2: in languages that mark gender on nouns, such as French, Spanish, and Bulgarian, it is easier to acquire the grammatical knowledge that nouns and adjective agree (gender agreement) than the idiosyncratic gender value of each noun, known as gender assignment.

Now, let's take this distinction between lexical and grammatical knowledge to a theoretical level, to a generalization that gets at the core of language variation. If UG is the common ground among languages, how do languages vary, and how is this variation delimited? One current view, known as the Borer–Chomsky Conjecture, is that variation is restricted to those possibilities that a language's functional inventory makes available. The linguist Hagit Borer articulated it in the following way: "The inventory of inflectional rules and of grammatical formatives in any given language is idiosyncratic and learned on the basis of input data" (Borer, 1984: 29). Within second language acquisition, Fukui's (1988) Functional Parameterization Hypothesis extends the Borer–Chomsky conjecture, proposing that only functional elements are subject to parametric variation. Viewed a slightly different way, we can say that parametric variation is restricted to functional elements in the lexicon (that is, instantiations of Complementizer, Agreement, Tense, etc.).

What does this mean in practice? Let's return to our English/Bulgarian examples. One way in which we can define the differences between these languages is that aspect is associated with particular features on a (functional) Aspect Phrase head. English has the value 'Mark aspect through the object quantization';[8] while Bulgarian has the value 'Mark aspect with a prefix on the

---

[8] A quantized expression is such that, whenever it is true of some entity, it is not true of any proper subparts of that entity. For example, if something is an apple then no proper subpart of that thing is

verb.' These different values constitute the grammatical information that must be acquired so that learners can reset how the Parameter of Aspect is valued. Other examples are the Nominal Agreement parameter, which is expressed through a feature on the nominal head (NP) or the *wh*-movement parameter, which is captured by a feature on the Complementizer Phrase (CP). Note that this information captured in functional features is distinct from the purely lexical information of, for example, what gender we attribute to each noun in languages like French, Spanish, or Bulgarian. Thus, the acquisition of a second language is successful when two conditions are met: when parameter values have been reset, and when all the associated lexical expressions have been memorized.

3.5 Input Effects in Bilinguals and Child L2 Learners

Unlike monolingual speakers, bilingual speakers can vary substantially in terms of the amount of exposure they receive in a given language. Not surprisingly, research has found that this variation is related to a bilingual's language capacities when producing or comprehending the language – a finding that is known as an "input effect." In this section, we will review some representative studies that have investigated input effects on bilingual children and child second language learners.

Bilingual children are exposed to two languages from birth, or within the first year of their lives.[9] In societies where two languages are regularly spoken in roughly equal measure, such as the province of Quebec in Canada, many children are exposed to both French and English in mixed language households. In order to study bilinguals' grammatical development, Elin Thordardottir (2015) examined the French and English of three- and five-year-old bilinguals who were exposed to these languages to varying degrees. Thordardottir then compared their language-specific development to that of monolingual children. Based on a parent questionnaire collecting information about the input that the children received over their lifetimes, children were divided into five exposure groups: Monolingual French, more French (where exposure to English ranged between 6 and 39 percent), equal French and English (40–60 percent English), more English (61–94 percent English), and monolingual English. Thordardottir then examined 100 utterances per child in each language (excluding imitations

---

an apple. Bare plurals (*houses*) and mass nouns (*water*) are non-quantized. Quantized objects mark telic predicates; non-quantized objects create atelic predicates.

[9] Researchers distinguish between simultaneous bilingualism (languages are learned at the same time) and sequential bilingualism (the second language is learned after the first). In this discussion, we use the term bilingual to mean simultaneous bilingual. Unfortunately, we cannot do justice to the comparisons between adult learners and child bilinguals in this short Element.

of parents or caregivers). In English, she documented accuracy for contracted verb forms, tense (regular and irregular past), 3rd person –*s*, progressive –*ing*, and noun inflections (plural and possessive –*s*). In French, accuracy was reported for verb person marking, verb tense, verb mood, gender (adjective and pronoun agreement with referent) and plural (plurals of nouns, adjectives, and pronouns other than personal pronouns). Thordardottir found that the amount of input children received in each language significantly impacted their grammatical development. Each language was learned in a highly language-specific manner, but closely mirroring the amount of exposure received in this language. That is, the children exposed to more English were better at English morphology, and they maintained that advantage in their development. Remarkably, both vocabulary and grammar were determined to depend to a similar extent on input.

The study described looks at acquisition of two languages from infancy. What if acquisition starting later works differently? The answer comes from another study focusing on input effects conducted by linguist Sharon Unsworth (Unsworth, 2016). Unsworth was interested in finding evidence for age and/or input effects across three different linguistic domains: morphosyntax, vocabulary, and syntax–semantics. To this end, she compared data from English-speaking children acquiring Dutch from two distinct groups: those whose age of onset to Dutch was between one and three years and, on the other hand, children whose age of onset was between four and seven years. The children were tested on their knowledge of verb morphology, V2 placement, vocabulary, and direct object scrambling. The latter construction involves an interpretive constraint on indefinite objects when these move over negation (the linguistic term is "scrambled," as in scrambled eggs).

Unsworth predicted that she would find both age and input effects in the domain of morphosyntax. In formulating this prediction, she followed Yang's idea that the V2 parameter (see previous) would be set later than four years of age. Why would that be the case? Because the crucial evidence – non-subject-initial sentences as in (2c) – are infrequent in the input, constituting less than 10 percent of relevant sentences. She also predicted that vocabulary acquisition would not depend on age because words are learned throughout the lifespan, but she did predict input effects. Finally, Unsworth argued that the semantic property she tested, the interpretive constraints on scrambling, represented a Poverty-of-the-Stimulus learning situation; therefore, no age or input effects were expected.

Unsworth found that there were *no age effects* between the two participant groups in any of these areas of the grammar. In other words, no matter whether the children started learning Dutch before or after the age of four, their

Table 1 Accuracy on verb morphology, verb placement, age-appropriate vocabulary, and scrambling (modified from Unsworth)

Property	Children with Age of Onset < 4	Children with Age of Onset > 4
Verb morphology		
– 3rd person singular	78%	70%
– 3rd person plural	88%	93%
Verb placement		
– after adverb	69%	48%
– after object	89%	80%
Vocabulary	90%	90%
Scrambling	90%	96%

Note: Scrambling refers to the accuracy of scrambled indefinite objects interpreted as specific.

development on the tested properties was comparable. Only one factor was significantly related to children's scores on verb placement (syntax), verb morphology, and vocabulary: their current amount of exposure to Dutch. That is, she established *input effects* for all these areas of the grammar. Notice also the interesting variation within a parameter: children are more accurate with V2 if the sentence starts with an object, as compared to when it begins with an adverb. The only property where exposure to input did not matter was scrambling. As the reader can verify from the last line in Table 1, all the children are highly accurate when tested on this semantic knowledge. This outcome is expected if, as Unsworth argued, scrambling represents a Poverty-of-the-Stimulus learning situation, meaning that it depends solely on F1 (UG). This comprehensive and carefully designed study makes a very clear case for F1 as well as F2 effects in child second language acquisition.

3.6 Input Effects in Adult Learners

Compared to child language acquisition, the field of SLA lacks corpora documenting L2 individual exposure over time (Rankin & Unsworth, 2016). This is because adult L2 learners are exposed to a much wider range of interlocutors, compared to children. Hence, input effects on rate of acquisition have not been studied longitudinally. If one wants to detect input effects in cross-sectional adult second language acquisition, the research design could be one of two types. First, one can compare learners exposed to different input on the same property and establish meaningful differences in rate and/or accuracy of acquisition. Second, one could compare acquisition of the same property in languages where input differs. In this section, we review two such studies. It is important to keep in mind that we are not talking about instruction effects but input effects. This means that we will be looking at properties that are not explicitly taught – at least not on a regular basis.

The first research design we mentioned can be exemplified by the study of Lydia White and Alan Juffs (White & Juffs, 1998), which focused on testing knowledge of *wh*-movement constraints by Chinese learners of English. Mandarin Chinese and English differ in this respect: while English *wh*-words move to the left reaches of the sentence, as in (6b), Chinese wh-words stay *in situ* (6a).

(6) a. *Hufei mai-le*   *shenme*   [Mandarin Chinese]
         Hufei buy-PERF   what
         'What did Hufei buy?'
     b. *What did John buy?*
     c. *What did you wonder whether John bought ____?   (*wh*-island)
     d. What did you wonder John bought ____?

What is more, long-distance *wh*-movement obeys very complicated constraints, illustrated partially by (6c,d), where the underlined section marks the original position of the *wh*-word, before moving to the left. Current linguistic analyses propose that the ungrammaticality of (6c) results from the *wh*-word *what* travelling too far from its original position (embedded object). Comparing (6c) and (6d) reveals that although *what* can actually move two clauses away from its embedded object position, it must stop over in the embedded CP position (above the subject), marked with a crossed-out *what*. The unacceptability of (6c) is then due to this position being occupied by *whether*. The crossed out, unpronounced *what* is called an intermediate trace or gap, and it has been argued that such constraints do not apply in languages without overt *wh*-movement, (e.g. Mandarin); as a result, knowledge of this constraint can only come through UG when Chinese learners acquire *wh*-movement in English.

White and Juffs (1998) compared the performance of two groups of Chinese learners: one which had never left China and another which was studying in Canada and was therefore exposed to naturalistic English input. As we can see, the authors were comparing learners who received very different types of input. The results of their investigation show that not only were the learners' judgments highly accurate, but also that the two groups were not statistically different, in spite of the differences in their exposure to English. Thus, the authors concluded that these intricate *wh*-movement constraints were "activated" without explicit knowledge or instruction.

Although White and Juffs did not find evidence of input effects, a study by Christos Pliatsikas and Theo Marinis points to possibly different input effects. Pliatsikas and Marinis (2013) investigated the processing of *wh*-phrases when these were extracted from relative clauses, as exemplified in (7). As before, the crossed out *wh*-word *who* indicates the sites through which it has moved on its way left (known as intermediate "gaps").

(7) *The manager [CP who_i the secretary claimed [CP that the new salesman had pleased]] will raise company salaries.*

The authors compared the performance of native speakers, advanced naturalistic speakers, and advanced classroom learners. However, even though both learner groups had comparable second language proficiency, only learners with naturalistic exposure were similar to native speakers when processing intermediate gaps, suggesting that linguistic immersion lead to native-like abstract syntactic processing. It is worth reminding the reader that, although both White and Juffs (1998) and Pliatsikas and Marinis (2013) investigate second language processing, their findings are reflective of the grammatical knowledge, or mental representations, of their participants. In summary, we have seen that in the area of complex syntax, naturalistic exposure may provide an input effect in processing.

A further study by Slabakova (2015) searched for input effects using meaning comprehension. In this study, input was quantified as the *frequency* with which a certain construction occurs, which gives us a proxy for how often learners may experience it in everyday communication. Slabakova (2015) utilized the second type of design mentioned (comparing acquisition outcomes of the same property in languages where input differs). The study tested the same constructions – topicalization (8a) and focus fronting (9b) – in Spanish and English, languages in which these constructions occur with different frequency. The study involved learners of English who were native Spanish speakers, and learners of Spanish who were English native speakers.

(8) a. [Context: *Did you like the wine?*]
The wine I didn't drink. I stuck to lemon ices.
b. [Context: *When did you sell that chair?*]
The TABLE I sold, not the chair.
c. [Context: I need to buy a newspaper and some bread.]
El periódico, lo comprará antes de ir al trabajo.
The newspaper CL.ACC buy.FUT.1SG before of go to-the work
'The newspaper, I will buy before work.'
d. [context: John bought the furniture]
LA ALFOMBRA compró (no los muebles)
the rug bought (not the furniture).
He bought THE RUG (not the furniture).

In these constructions, objects can move to the left periphery of the sentence if it has already been mentioned (8a) or is new and contrastive information (8b). Spanish topicalization (known as clitic left dislocation) is somewhat similar in form to this other fronting operation, with one morphological difference: the moved object has to be doubled by a clitic (8c). This is not true for focus fronting (8d). Corpus data ascertained that topicalization in Spanish is about 100 times more frequent than it is in English. Table 2, modified from Slabakova's (2015) table 6, plots predictions based on L1 transfer and input frequency, compared to actual accuracy findings. Topicalization is predicted to be hard if native language transfer is the decisive factor for successful acquisition, since Spanish and English have a morphological difference, the clitic doubling. Focus fronting, on the other hand, is not morphologically different in English and Spanish. Finally, based on which construction is more frequent, second language learners of Spanish should enjoy an advantage when learning topicalization. In the end, none of these predictions were completely supported.

Examining Table 2, the learner can determine that transfer from the native language played a critical role, in the sense that it allowed all the English L2 learners to be accurate on focus fronting, but it could not account for the successful acquisition of Spanish topicalization. Experience-based predictions suggest the more frequent constructions should be acquired faster and more accurately, since they are encountered more often. However, taken in isolation, experience (as an explanation) also came up short because focus fronting was acquired successfully, even though it is as rare in the input as is topicalization. Slabakova concluded that native transfer could account for all the findings in

Table 2 Predictions and actual results on topicalization and focus fronting in English and Spanish, following Slabakova (2015)

Construction	Predictions based on L1 transfer	Predictions based on input frequency	Actual results
Topicalization in L2 English	Hard	Hard	Failure
Topicalization in L2 Spanish (CLLD)	Hard	Easy	Success
Focus fronting in L2 English	Easy	Hard	Success
Focus fronting in L2 Spanish	Easy	Easy	Success

their complexity, but only when considered alongside experience. And this is a fitting conclusion to this section as well: Input works in tandem with mother-tongue influence in L2 acquisition.

3.7 What Can't the Input Give the Learner?

Finally, let's consider the upper limits of what experience can provide for learners. As we know, the bulk of language acquisition consists of coupling form and meaning, and establishing this mapping in mental representation to be accessed and used in communication. Yet there are some linguistic properties where two meanings are aligned with one form, or else analogy suggests that a couple of meanings should exist, but one of them is not available. We discussed these Poverty-of-the-Stimulus learning situations earlier as representing limits of experience because we have evidence that learners demonstrate knowledge that cannot come from the input. Some of the best-known examples of this situation come from scope effects, as in (9), following Marsden (2009). Example (9) shows that one sentence string accommodates two meanings. The *subject-wide scope* S > O corresponds to the surface word order and is preferred by speakers because it is easier to compute. The inverse *object-wide scope*, O > S, also known as the *distributive reading*, is harder to get for English native speakers, although not impossible if the context is sufficiently clear.

(9) *Someone read every book.*
     S > O: There is some person x, such that x read every book.
     O > S: For each book y, some person or other read y.

Crucially for this study, the distributive reading is not available for the Korean and Japanese sentence equivalents. These languages scramble the object over the subject to get that reading. As Marsden (2009) argued, the absence of object-wide scope in the SOV Japanese sentence constitutes a Poverty-of-the-Stimulus situation for English learners of Japanese, since their own SVO sentences allow such scope. Marsden's experimental study showed that very advanced learners of Japanese were able to develop target-like knowledge of the absence of inverse scope, even though evidence for it was absent in the input. Recall also that Unsworth's (2016) child learners of Dutch acquired the interpretation of scrambled indefinite objects with very high accuracy. Coupled with the study by Martohardjono (1993) that we reviewed in Section 1, these studies chart the limits of experience (F2) and provide evidence for F1, Universal Grammar, being active in L2 acquisition.

At the same time, there are some properties that are amply modeled in the input, yet learners experience them as a challenge, and error rates may be higher than accuracy rates. A prime example is the functional morpheme –*s* marking agreement between the subject and the verb in English (e.g. *He walk-s*). This morpheme is extremely frequent in the input. It appears in all simple present tense sentences that have a 3rd-person subject. In the 520-million-word *Corpus of Contemporary American English* (COCA, Corpus.bya.edu, 2018), the 3rd person singular –*s* occurs a total of 6,198,523 times or 37.5 percent of all present-tense lexical verbs and in 10.1 percent of all lexical verbs. At the same time, learners routinely drop this marking when producing language. Furthermore, some learners, such as Chinese native speakers (Lardiere, 1998a, 1998b), drop it more than others. For example, Lardiere's (1998a, 1998b) subject Patty produces the –*s* 4.5 percent of the time. Why would that be? The Missing Surface Inflection Hypothesis (Haznedar, 2001; Haznedar & Schwartz, 1997; Prévost & White, 2000a, 2000b; White, 2003) provides one explanation of this robust acquisition observation based on lexical competition and default morpheme insertion. The Contextual Complexity Hypothesis (Hawkins & Casillas, 2008) attributes the low rates of this morpheme's production to the complexity of the featural contexts required for its insertion. Processability Theory (Pienemann, 1998) suggests that feature unification, (i.e. the exchange of information between verb and noun), is challenging, while Input Processing (VanPatten, 1996) explains that learners prefer to process lexical items, not functional morphemes. In sum, explanations abound for the low accuracy of learners with this functional morpheme; the main observation is that high input frequency alone does not guarantee easy acquisition.

3.8 Conclusion

In this section, we focused on a specific implication for SLA related to the second factor of language design (input) because acquisition without experiencing language is unthinkable. As many generative studies have shown, differential experience of a certain grammatical morpheme or construction alters the acquisition path and rate. At the same time, learners make very specific, feature-related errors that are difficult to explain based on salience and frequency. They also demonstrate knowledge without experience in Poverty-of-the-Stimulus learning situations. Thus, learners both know more than what is in the input and do not produce everything that is modeled by the input. Finally, when we investigate input (F2) limitations, UG (F1), the native language, and computational complexity (F3) assert their significance as factors determining SLA.

4 What Are the Implications for Pedagogy?

4.1 GenSLA Research and Language Pedagogy

The study of second language acquisition is a worthwhile endeavor for at least two reasons, according to Rosamond Mitchell and colleagues (Mitchell, Myles,

& Marsden, 2013). The first is that knowing about second language acquisition can promote our knowledge about the nature of language, human learning, and the mind's architecture. The second reason is more practical in nature: if we have a sophisticated understanding of the second language acquisition process, we could help the world's instructors and learners who are struggling with teaching and acquiring, respectively, a second language. Since this is a good and noble aim, we explore here some of the pedagogical implications we can derive from the generative study of SLA. We hope to show that, although pedagogical aims have not always been central to the generative framework, the time is ripe for Generative SLA researchers to consider pedagogical aims because these are beneficial for both researchers and teachers. Before proceeding, however, a couple of cautionary notes are needed.

The primary goals of GenSLA research and of language pedagogy exist independently and, not surprisingly, differ from each other in non-trivial respects. Generative second language researchers aim to understand the nature of the learner's linguistic competence, while language teachers aim to find the most efficient pedagogical tools to help learners acquire language. Thus, although findings from one field can, in principle, inform the other, this cannot always be the case because understanding that a particular construction is difficult to learn doesn't necessarily offer a clearer path for how to teach it. This idea is hardly new; Lydia White has aptly noted that even when researchers can arrive at an understanding of the learners' competence, this knowledge will not necessarily translate into insights for teaching (White, 2018b). Finally, we must note that while GenSLA research has considerable potential to offer pedagogical insights, we must also recognize the vast literature on instructed SLA, which has been the primary source of data-driven advancement in the field of second language pedagogy. In this sense, what we advocate for here is combining the myriad insights from instructed SLA research with a more nuanced understanding of structure, which GenSLA researchers can offer.

Cautionary notes aside, we are interested in exploring those research outcomes that can provide useful insights for language teachers and learners. Again, we do not mean to replace the insights of instructed SLA research, but to build on these results and provide further avenues of research. We are hardly alone in pursuing this aim. Two recent journal issues (one in *Language Teaching Research*, another in *Instructed Second Language Acquisition*) have focused on these connections, and these explorations have resulted in important insights. For instance, the researchers Stefano Rastelli and Kook-Hee Gil (Rastelli & Gil, 2018) have offered several recommendations to guide a fruitful collaboration between research in the GenSLA tradition and Applied Linguistics as a whole. Their recommendations include that GenSLA should (a) explore additional insights from the Minimalist Program (Chomsky, 1995), (b) use concepts, methodologies, and techniques of statistical and cognitive investigation typically used beyond the generative field, as well as (c) shift from investigating the teaching of grammar rules to other important factors in language teaching. Before catching further glimpses into GenSLA's future, we will first take a short walk down memory lane and explore some of the past connections between GenSLA and pedagogy, since these connections are not new.

4.2 Missed or Gained Opportunities: The Role of Negative Evidence

There is little debate in the field of SLA regarding the importance of second language input, or what is called *positive evidence,* because no acquisition is possible without it. One enduring question in the second language teaching profession, however, is the manner in which instructors should react in the face of learners' errors. Should teachers provide corrections when learners produce forms that are not native-like? In other words, should the teacher provide the learner with *negative evidence,* or explicit instruction of what is not possible in a given language?

In the last three decades, the pendulum has swung both in favor of and against providing learners with corrections, with a number of empirical investigations showing support for and against negative evidence. In this section, we will talk about one early GenSLA investigation (White, 1991) whose findings had a deep influence on the field and which might have led to somewhat premature conclusions about whether or not to provide negative evidence. To talk about this study, we need to explore the acquisition of English by French speakers, specifically, the acquisition of the syntax of adverbs because these have different placement restrictions in the two languages.

One important difference between French and English is that French allows word orders which are ungrammatical in English, and English, likewise, allows options that are ruled out in French. Specifically, English accepts SAVO (subject-adverb-verb-object) orders, as we can see in sentences such as *Mary often watches television*, while the French equivalent is not a valid string (**Marie souvent regarde la télévision*). Conversely, the order SVAO is licit in French (*Marie regarde souvant la télévision*) but not in English (**Mary watches often television*). White focused on this distinction and investigated whether instruction that provides negative evidence (corrections) would lead to French speakers ruling out the ungrammatical English strings.

White's investigation was very thorough and used a variety of instruments. It also included a clear pedagogical intervention, which was administered to an experimental group. She measured the outcomes of an additional experimental group (which we will not discuss here), and a control group, which did not receive negative input. Without discussing all the particulars of the study, we should note that the intervention was administered three months into an English-as-a-second-language program. The experimental group focusing on adverbs received instruction for two weeks. Instruction consisted of "intensive work on adverb placement," including activities that focused on adverb meanings. Immediately after this form-focused instruction period, the learners were tested. They also completed a delayed post-test a year after instruction. The results provided support for explicit instruction including negative evidence in the immediate post-test, suggesting that some constructions cannot be learned from positive evidence alone. Unfortunately for negative-evidence enthusiasts, however, the results failed to provide support for negative evidence in the post-test that was administered a year later. From these results, White concluded that the intervention did not have lasting effects, which she interpreted as meaning that the intervention "did not in fact result in significant changes in the learners' underlying competence" (White, 1991: 158).

Following this and other studies, many GenSLA researchers steered clear of investigating pedagogical interventions, assuming, based on these and other similar results, that negative evidence was not universally effective. Recall that, as we mentioned at the outset of the section, the goals of GenSLA are independent of pedagogy, so this lack of involvement is not completely surprising. Within the instructed SLA research community, however, research on explicit correction flourished and yielded many interesting findings. A research-synthesis article by Roehr-Bracking (2015) shows, from a usage-based perspective, that explicit instruction is indeed positively related to many aspects of L2 proficiency.

How can we compare the results of White's investigation with results such as those presented in Roehr-Bracking? First, we must bear in mind that the results supporting explicit instruction focus on a great variety of grammatical constructions and language pairings, such that it is hard to apply these results to every instructional context. Moreover, we must consider the myriad factors that can impact the effectiveness of pedagogical interventions because different pedagogical approaches (e.g. task-based language teaching vs. form-focused teaching) or the length of the intervention can yield distinct outcomes. Thus, our main point here is not to question the research outcomes of either investigation but to suggest that GenSLA researchers could work in tandem with instructional SLA researchers to investigate the effectiveness of pedagogical interventions. For instance, it is possible that the instructional delivery in White's study can be improved upon, or that two weeks of instruction are insufficient to bring about significant changes in grammatical competence. As suggested by Schwartz and Gubala-Ryzak (1992), it could be the case that the teaching intervention did not engage UG at all and that these learners learnt something superficial which they later forgot. In any case, these are interesting empirical questions that research can answer. Our position is that these collaborations (GenSLA and instructed SLA research) can be very fruitful and advance our understanding of the acquisition and learning processes in ways that can positively impact pedagogical practices.

4.3 Determining Where the Difficulties Lie in Acquisition

Generative linguists have proposed specific hypotheses about how grammar is organized in a speaker's mind and have investigated the nature of what is typically known as *language architecture*. Although generative second language research has not typically been undertaken with pedagogical concerns at the forefront, this knowledge can nonetheless help us determine several useful particulars with respect to second language acquisition. These insights include the answers to questions such as: What type of input can help a learner re-structure their grammar? What aspects of the L2 grammar will be especially difficult to acquire (based, for instance, on a given speaker's first language)? What aspects of the L1 grammar will be especially difficult to overcome, especially when the input can be misleading or hard to find? In what follows, we present several examples in which generative SLA researchers have attempted to answer such questions and, in so doing, have offered insights that can be useful to L2 pedagogy.

4.3.1 The Conversation about Comprehensible Input

The field of second language pedagogy has undergone significant changes in the last hundred years. While generative scholars have not typically been significant contributors to these changes, and rightly so, many potential connections between linguistic theory and teaching and learning second languages were explored early on. In fact, some of these insights have driven important conversations in the second language teaching profession. As a first example, we will discuss a construct that has been highly influential in pedagogy: the construct of *comprehensible input*. But first, a bit of context is needed.

In the earlier part of the last century, the dominant pedagogical approach to teaching second languages was the so-called Grammar-Translation Method. As its name suggests, learners were expected to translate written passages (often literary). Lessons were centered on the acquisition of vocabulary and on reviewing (comparative) grammar points, studying the structural rules in each language and exploring exceptions. Following the previous section, it shouldn't be surprising to discover that this approach was not particularly successful in terms of developing fluent second language speakers. Other pedagogical approaches that also focused on acquiring sentence patterns, such as the Audio-Lingual Method, were popular at the start of the second half of the century, but were eventually superseded by other pedagogical approaches, in no small part because learners did not typically end up being fluent.

As you may imagine, this common finding was frustrating for language teachers: Even if learners could correctly use structures in the classroom, they could not consistently perform basic language *functions* (such as apologizing, inviting or declining invitations, etc.). Worse still, this was the case *even* when learners could demonstrate knowledge of the necessary grammatical rules in tests. The central insight that emerged from this era was that learners needed not only to possess the requisite linguistic competence but also to attain communicative competence (Hymes, 1972). Consequently, many teachers thought that the development of communicative competence should be the goal of language teaching.

Many language teachers and scholars also embraced proposals put forward by educational researcher Stephen Krashen. One of these suggested that learners could progress in their development (proceeding from stage to stage to match native norms) if and when those learners received input just above what they could comprehend, a notion operationalized as $i+1$ and termed the *Input Hypothesis* (Krashen, 1982). To explain what this means, we follow Lydia White (White, 1987), who illustrated it in this way: we could think of "i" as roughly representing the learner's system without a certain grammatical feature/structure (to wit, the current level of linguistic competence of the learner), while $i+1$ represents the next level in the grammar, a level including the missing grammatical feature or structure. How could learners advance to the next stage in acquisition, then? Under Krashen's view, acquisition could proceed straightforwardly if learners received "comprehensible" input, granted that external barriers, such as the affective filter, could be lowered.

Krashen's ideas were popular in teaching circles, but White was skeptical about the necessity of limiting the learner's input to that deemed comprehensible. She viewed simplification of input as potentially problematic, and to explain her reasoning, she presented a hypothetical case of a second language learner who had not acquired the passive yet and who, consequently, would not have been able to correctly interpret a sentence such as *John was kissed by Mary*. Without a passive rule, it is possible to assume (consciously or not), based on word order alone, that the kisser in this situation was John, rather than Mary. In this case, while the interpretation is incorrect, it is plausible because both John and Mary are capable of performing the action of kissing.

Some sentences discourage such ambiguity despite their syntactic similarities to the one presented above. For instance, what would happen if a learner encounters a sentence such as *The book is read by John*? In this case, White reasoned, real-world plausibility stands in the way because books cannot read people – an interpretation one could formulate by following word order alone. White argued that, in this case, it is actually the *incomprehensibility* of the input that can drive interlanguage development. In other words, far from needing input that is comprehensible (which might not lead to learners re-structuring their L1 grammars), learners need to encounter incomprehensible strings. Thus, White suggests that if learners' grammars do not include a certain rule, comprehensible input is not always apposite: in this case, the way forward was to provide the learner with incomprehensible input so that they would be forced to reanalyze the string and make sense of it.

4.3.2 Examining Teaching Materials

Another way in which generative linguists have sought links between research and pedagogy is by examining the input that learners receive. This research has resulted in interesting findings. Here we will explore only two cases (L2 textbooks presenting misleading input, and cases where certain constructions appear to be mostly absent from the input learners receive).

Misleading Rules in L2 Textbooks

As we have seen, linguists have arrived at nuanced descriptions of linguistic phenomena, many of which have been linked to features of human language in general. Unfortunately, however, this body of work has not always informed the contents of language textbooks, which often present grammar as a set of rules to be followed. These rules are often fairly general and sometimes not only fail to acknowledge important exceptions but, on occasion, actually misrepresent the way linguistic structures work. Inaccurate presentations can be especially misleading when native speakers of the language produce strings that contradict said rules – at times frequently so. Not surprisingly, the difference between how language textbooks present the rules and how native speakers use the structures has been the subject of several generative investigations.

In Section 2, we reviewed the case of the acquisition of object pronouns in French, which is often tricky for English speakers. Recall that English direct object pronouns encode the feature [±human] as well as biological gender (this is evident when examining the pronouns *him, her, it*).[10] Earlier, we talked about the acquisition of French direct object *clitic* pronouns (pronominal forms phonologically bound to another word). Now, let's focus on *strong pronouns* in French, when they are used as the complements of prepositions. One example would be the pronoun *lui* (him) in a French sentence such as *Je pense à lui* 'I think about him'. These pronouns are interesting because there seems to exist a mismatch between how they are presented to learners in second language textbooks and how French native speakers actually use and interpret them.

How can we know what French speakers do in this case? One way would be to let the specialists do the heavy lifting and turn to linguistic descriptions. However, in this particular case, this strategy won't work because linguists are split on the subject. Shimanskaya (2018) reported that while some linguists argue that French strong pronouns can take only [+human] or [+animate] antecedents, others have left the metaphorical door open to referents that are inanimate (hence, [–human], [–animate]), even though these pronouns might not be the most frequently chosen options, perhaps because there are four other ways to refer to inanimate referents in French. In any case, because of this debate in the literature, one must look outside of linguistic descriptions to find out what French native speakers do. And this is exactly what Shimanskaya did. She turned to two different methods to find out how native speakers of French interpret strong pronouns. First, she conducted an experimental study with native speakers of French wherein she verified, using a task where speakers selected referents from among different picture options, whether these pronouns could refer to both human *and* inanimate referents. Second, she inspected a corpus to ascertain whether French native speakers would use these pronouns when referring to inanimate objects as well as humans. Finally, she examined French L2 language textbooks in order to determine whether they followed native speaker usage.

The results of the corpus study and the experimental study pointed in the same direction: native speakers of French can and do use strong pronoun complements of prepositions to refer to inanimate referents, even if these instances are less frequent than alternative encodings. Notably, however, Shimanskaya's inspection of L2 materials yielded an opposite view: the textbooks she inspected did not mention or allow for this possibility and suggested, instead, that only [+human] referents (and, in one case, [+animate] referents) were available with these pronouns. So, while these textbook grammar rules captured many of the cases where these pronouns refer to people, they failed to

---

[10] Number is also encoded, but we are limiting our discussion to 3rd-person singular pronouns here.

account for some of the sentences that French speakers produced and interpreted – the sentences in which the pronouns were used to refer to inanimate objects. Here's the kicker: while her study determined that second language learners can, eventually, acquire these distinctions, it stands to reason that it would be helpful to present accurate descriptions in the textbooks to aid in the acquisition process. Currently, learners must ignore the dutiful textbook descriptions if they are to behave as native speakers do.

The Case of the Missing Input

For many classroom learners, the main source of L2 evidence is the input that is provided in institutional settings, be it via textbook materials or "teacher talk." If we want to understand how this input affects acquisition, it makes sense to examine these input sources. Examining the input can help us to determine whether the absence or presence of a certain linguistic property can explain successful acquisition of said property (or else, lack of success in this area).

Here, we will look at one such example of research doing exactly that, which focused on the acquisition of Spanish as a second language. Spanish, unlike rigid word-order languages like English, is fairly flexible when it comes to how words are ordered in a sentence, even though the canonical order is Subject-Verb-Object. As we saw previously, one of the common word-order permutations we can find in Spanish is that native speakers typically move a phrase to the left in what is called a clitic left dislocation (CLLD). Remember that this structure involves topics – that is, phrases that have been previously mentioned – that show up at the far-left edge of the sentence. Additionally, also remember that the dislocated phrase is doubled by a clitic that agrees with the phrase in cases where the moved phrase is an object.

If you have ever attempted to learn a second language in a classroom context, you probably know that the immediate concerns of learners are learning vocabulary and grammar (by which we often mean morphology and syntax). In contrast, the distinction that regulates the presence or absence of a clitic in CLLD, which depends on the discourse context, appears to be pretty minute. The obvious question is: How do language learners acquire this minute distinction? Or, perhaps more importantly, do they acquire it at all?

This was the focus of our previous collaborative work, and, in order to answer these questions, we first determined whether learners could tell whether the clitic was needed or not, depending on the context (Leal, 2018b; Slabakova, Kempchinsky, & Rothman, 2012). As it turns out, they could, and, in fact, second language learners were quite successful at it, especially as they increased in proficiency. Then we tested their knowledge of this construction using a methodology that measured the time it took for learners to react to sentences with and without a clitic in a context where the clitic was needed (Leal et al., 2017). Again, our learners showed that they could distinguish between these two types of sentences because they read the sentences *without* the clitic more slowly than the sentences *with* the clitic, suggesting that clitics were indeed expected, given the context.

However, we did find that learning this construction took a long time (over a decade or more of exposure to Spanish), which was a bit surprising. Another interesting finding was that learners who had study-abroad experience were quicker to learn this distinction. Even more curiously, length of exposure to Spanish in the classroom did not correlate with acquisition of this structure – something we would have expected. This finding piqued our curiosity: Could it be that this structure was not taught in the classroom, explaining perhaps why it took so long for learners to acquire it?

To answer this question, we used three different methodologies (Leal & Slabakova, 2019). First, we asked second language Spanish teachers, in Mexico and the USA, whether they taught the structure and whether they could determine that it was, indeed, grammatical. This inquiry showed us that although all teachers accepted the structure as part of their grammar, they did not teach it in their classes. Reasons varied, but many teachers thought the structure was "informal" or unworthy of classroom instruction. Second, we examined textbook materials for examples of the construction. This exploration yielded very few exemplars of the construction and virtually no explanations that involved discourse or other descriptions about the linguistic context, showing that students were rarely exposed to this construction in the classroom via textbooks. Finally, we recorded around five hours of classroom instruction (across three different classes) in advanced Spanish-content courses. What we found was that the rate of production of this structure was lower than the rates reported in native-speaker corpora (Slabakova, 2015). In other words, it corroborated our initial sense that part of the issue with the acquisition of dislocations in Spanish was related to instructional practices: students who did study abroad would have been exposed to the higher frequency rate of this structure "in the wild," so to speak, while the input that instructed learners received was somewhat impoverished in this respect.

What should we conclude from these studies? Straightforwardly, these investigations have revealed a few specific ways in which instructional materials could be improved. First, GenSLA researchers could contribute to the refinement of textbooks by pointing out rules that fail to reflect native-speaker usage, following Shimanskaya's example. Second, GenSLA researchers could also detect areas where the input of learners is unnecessarily reduced, as in the case of dislocations in Spanish. While these avenues are potentially fruitful, we again highlight that these findings serve as a complement to instructed SLA research because the substantial advancements made in that area must not be disregarded. In what follows, we explore an example of further collaboration between instructed SLA research and GenSLA research that could be advantageous for the field.

4.4 Conclusion

We have argued here that GenSLA researchers have provided us with a nuanced view of the language architecture – a view that, in turn, can be used to delimit what is easy and what is hard to learn in a second language. We have also suggested, following others (Whong, Gil, & Marsden, 2013), that these insights have the potential to be translated into linguistically principled second language pedagogical practices. Finally, we have also proposed that GenSLA researchers should work hand-in-hand with instructional SLA researchers to investigate the efficacy of pedagogical practices as these pertain to specific linguistic structures, so that we can provide teachers and learners with efficient teaching tools.

5 What Are the New Avenues for Research?

In the preceding sections of this Element, we presented theoretical models of how GenSLA scholars think about *challenges* in the transition from one state of L2 knowledge to another, as predicted by the property theory, generative linguistics. Such current models include the Feature Reassembly Hypothesis, the Interface Hypothesis, the Interpretability Hypothesis, and the Bottleneck Hypothesis. Without a doubt, these models will be tested with new properties and new language combinations in the future. With this in mind, the current section focuses on an exciting area of growth within GenSLA research: L2 development and the transition theories that explain it.

5.1 Transition Theories of Development

The question of development is hardly new, as it has been subject to extensive debate in the field of first language acquisition. In fact, it has been studied from a variety of perspectives, including input-driven (Tomasello, 2000; Goldberg, 2006) and knowledge-driven approaches (Chomsky, 1965; Pinker, 1989; Viau & Lidz, 2011). Input-driven approaches claim that linguistic interactions give rise to emergent linguistic forms (Elman et al., 1996). The learned knowledge (the acquired linguistic information) is thought to be a compressed memory of the patterns encountered in the input, such that recently encountered input activates previously encountered input through a form of similarity measure. Knowledge-driven approaches, on the other hand, postulate that the learner analyzes the input in search of cues that are used to establish abstract representations. Parts of these representations are said to be innate and determine the cues that learners use to select them (Fodor, 1998a, 1998b; Lightfoot, 1999).

One reason why this has become a growing area in GenSLA studies is that much less is known about how linguistic development proceeds in second language acquisition. Historically, GenSLA research has focused on property-based theories and, until very recently, had largely overlooked transition theories, one notable exception being the work of Susanne Carroll (2001, 2007) (Gregg, 2003; White, 2018: 58). However, this situation has changed and we have seen an increase in the number of hypotheses accounting for how second language learners develop from one state of linguistic knowledge to the next. These hypotheses have, in large part, been motivated by our expanding knowledge of how learners process language during real-time comprehension and how processing routines differ between first and second language speakers.

Psycholinguists Roger van Gompel and Martin Pickering (2007) have noted that research on language processing has typically been divided into two distinct camps: modular models, which postulate that the processing of morpho-syntax, semantics, and discourse are separate and in sequence, and interactive models, positing integration of all relevant sources of information at the same time. Interactive (also known as constraint-based models) "assume that the processor immediately draws upon all possible sources of information during sentence processing, including semantics, discourse context, and information about the frequency of syntactic structures (van Gompel & Pickering 2007: 292). In this section, we focus on second language development, studying it from a generative perspective. Readers interested in an example of a non-modular, emergentist model are encouraged to consult O'Grady (2005).

5.2 Theoretical Preliminaries

Before examining second language development, let's discuss the notion of learnability in the first language. Learnability issues have been debated extensively in the field of generative linguistics, crystalized in the logical problem of language acquisition. To refresh the reader's memory, the argument goes that language acquisition is aided by innate knowledge of linguistic principles, as well as knowledge of the possible variation (parameter values). Although generative linguists have largely adopted the Minimalist framework, the underlying concepts of Principles and Parameters remain fundamental to modern-day generative linguistics and several influential proposals of how parameter setting proceeds have been advanced over the years, including Robin Clark's (1990, 1992) General Algorithm, Edward Gibson and Kenneth Wexler's (Gibson & Wexler, 1994) Triggering Learning Algorithm, Charles Yang's Variational Learning Model (Yang, 2002), and Janet Fodor's Parsing-to-Learn Hypothesis (Fodor, 1998a, 1998b). While these models diverge from each other in multiple ways, they all stand in contradistinction to Chomsky's (1981) initial triggering model (Gibson & Wexler, 1994; Fodor & Sakas, 2017). To wit, these models describe learning as a process wherein learners analyze entire grammars until they arrive at one that is compatible with the properties of the target language.

Fodor's (1998a, 1998b) Parsing-to-Learn Hypothesis, the seminal view of generative psycholinguistics, starts from the idea that mechanical parameter setting does not sufficiently account for how this process unfolds. "Sentences must be parsed to discover the properties that select between parameter values" (Fodor, 1998b: 339). She proposed the view that the human sentence-processing system (the parser) plays a crucial role in learning and suggests that a "special-purpose acquisition algorithm" is not needed as a further explanation (Fodor, 1998b: 341). Instead, she argues that the parser is fully innate and universal to the extent that language-specific parsing routines do not exist.[11] Under this view, the parametric values of the input grammar are available from UG prior to a learner being exposed to the input, and exposure allows them to choose, or set, the value needed.

Fodor and colleagues conceptualize parameter values as UG-sanctioned "treelets." A treelet (a small syntactic tree) represents a combination of under-specified syntactic nodes. To understand what this means, we can use one of the examples that Fodor offers. Let us then consider a treelet consisting of a verb phrase node, with verb and prepositional phrase as its daughters. If speakers had a treelet such as this, they could parse a string such as "Look at the frog." Conversely, a grammar that did not include such a treelet would fail to parse the sentence. Fodor proposes that learners use innate parametric treelets to salvage a parse of new input when this parse fails due to the absence of the relevant parameter value. Furthermore, the hypothesis suggests that parsing failures trigger the creation of a new parameter value. Thus, in this model, differences in sentence-parsing routines are attributed not to language-specific parsing routes per se, but rather to the different grammars that sustain parsing.

What are the practical consequences of this view for language acquisition? Following Fodor's insights, for learners to acquire a new grammar, they must first parse it by applying a supergrammar, or the 'best' grammar to which the

---

[11] For a discussion on the interaction between the grammar and parser, see Lewis and Phillips (2014).

learner has access: the grammar that contains the current grammar as well as all the UG-sanctioned properties. If the supergrammar can successfully parse the input sentence, then the learner processes the input in the same manner as an adult native speaker would. However, in the event of processing failure, the learner must access "the store of parametric treelets that UG makes available, seeking one that can bridge the gap in the parser tree" (Fodor & Sakas, 2017: 266). How does learning proceed, then? If we view learning as incremental, then each time a learner successfully parses a sentence using a new treelet, the treelet itself will be more activated (a psycholinguist would say that the activation threshold level of the treelet in question has been raised). This process will repeat itself until the treelet is added to the grammar. Some researchers question the notion that parametric treelets are innately specified. However, this issue forms part of a much broader question – whether knowledge of language is innate – which we discuss in Sections 1 and 3.

Within the second language literature, researchers make an important distinction between input and intake. Susan Gass (1988) has defined input as a process, involving mental psycholinguistic activity, by which linguistic material is assimilated before being incorporated into the learner's grammar. Under Fodor's approach, however, not all input equals intake. As Carroll (2017) points out, Fodor's (1998a, 1998b) work emphasized the importance of establishing a principled distinction between two input types: input-to-language-processors and input-to-the-language-acquisition-mechanisms. The former refers to "bits of the speech signal that are fed into language processors and which will be analyzable if the current state of the grammar permits it," whereas the latter concerns "what it is that those mechanisms need to create a novel representation" (Carroll, 2017: 5). At the outset of acquisition, we would expect to see a significant mismatch between the two types of input, such that input-to-the-language-acquisition-mechanisms would not be an accurate reflection of the linguistic environment. Carroll (2001) refers to this distinction as the difference between input and intake, respectively.

Over the years, other psycholinguists have used the input/intake distinction to develop a nuanced picture of second language development. Within this discussion, many researchers further appeal to the notion of the "inferential engine," a term that suggests that UG-constrained grammars generate expectations about what the learner should encounter in the input (Fodor; 1998b; Lidz & Gagliardi, 2015; Lightfoot, 1991; Pearl & Lidz, 2009; Regier & Gahl, 2003; Tenenbaum & Griffiths, 2001; VanPatten, 1996; Yang, 2002). For instance, Geffrey Lidz and Annie Gagliardi (Lidz & Gagliardi, 2015) propose a model in which intake is generated as a result of a comparison between the predicted features (as hypothesized by UG) and the perceptual representation (the actual input).

This comparison allows learners to generate inferences about grammatical features so that they can build a target grammar with properties that have not been encountered in input yet. These inferences consequently lead the learner to revise their current grammatical knowledge and add new features to, or modify existing features of, the developing interlanguage grammar.

5.3 Processing in L2 Acquisition

As we know, the outcomes from second language acquisition can vary significantly when compared to the outcomes from first language acquisition. Owing to a host of factors, outcomes vary among individual learners as well. In recent years, several researchers have proposed processing-based explanations to account for these differences. Much of this work has focused on processing as a means of extracting the meaning of utterances (Cunnings, 2017; cf., Clahsen & Felser, 2006, 2018), as opposed to processing as a mechanism for acquisition. In the first part of this section, we discuss processing-based explanations for first- and second language acquisition differences, focusing on the Shallow Structure Hypothesis and the Reduced Ability to Generate Expectations Hypothesis. Then, we explore several unified frameworks that combine both representational and processing accounts from a generative perspective. These frameworks can be broadly divided into two camps: failure-driven approaches and acquisition as a by-product of processing approaches.

5.3.1 Processing-for-Meaning Explanations

The Shallow Structure Hypothesis (SSH) (Clahsen & Felser, 2006, 2018) represents one of the most discussed and tested models of second language mental representations. Integrating linguistic theory and psycholinguistic principles, the model argues that second language learners, even highly proficient ones, experience persistent difficulties "building or manipulating abstract syntactic representations in real-time" and give preference to semantic or pragmatic information, unlike what native speakers do (Clahsen & Felser, 2018: 3). Thus, the SSH maintains that second language construct meaning by using lexical-semantic and/or pragmatic information or strategies that depend on argument structure due to second language learners' insufficiently detailed grammatical representations.

Early evidence supporting the SSH came from studies showing that, although second language learners were sensitive to semantic and pragmatic cues during processing, they constructed less-detailed syntactic representations when resolving syntactic ambiguities (Felser, Roberts, Marinis & Gross, 2003; Papadopoulou & Clahsen, 2003) and linguistic dependencies

(Felser & Roberts 2007; Marinis et al., 2005). Other studies investigating the processing of morphology also found that second language learners exhibit target-like priming behavior for derived word forms but not for inflected forms[12] (Kirkici & Clahsen, 2013; Jacob, Heyer, & Veríssimo, 2018) and that lexical, but not morphological, restrictions on word-formation processes modulate both first and second language processing in the same way (Clahsen et al., 2013, 2015).

The SSH has sparked lively debates. Opponents argue that first and second language sentence processing routines are closely aligned, and that differences between first and second language outcomes should be attributed, instead, to reduced lexical access or limited cognitive resources (McDonald, 2006; Hopp, 2006, 2010). It is also worth noting that the concept of shallow processing has important implications for failure-driven, grammar revision approaches, as we will see later (Dekydtspotter, Schwartz, & Sprouse, 2006, p. 36).

Another processing-for-meaning model, the Reduced Ability to Generate Expectations (RAGE) hypothesis (Grüter, Rohde, & Schafer, 2017) contends that second language learners' processing difficulties result from learners' limited ability, rather than inability, to generate expectations about upcoming linguistic information. Specifically, these differences in processing are expected to be more pronounced at the discourse level, where information from the context has to be integrated with the utterance being processed. At this point, however, the empirical evidence for this hypothesis remains mixed. Some studies have found evidence to suggest that L2 speakers are unable to actively predict upcoming information (Dallas, 2008; Kaan, Dallas, & Wijnen, 2010; Marinis et al., 2005), whereas others have found target-like predictive processing among L2 learners (Dussias et al., 2013; Hopp, 2013).

A common feature of both models is that they aim to explain deficiencies in second language outcomes, but do not detail how successful parsing and, ultimately, learning itself, actually happens. Next, we turn to these issues, which other theories address.

5.3.2 Unified Transition Theories

Unified frameworks that combine representational and processing accounts of learning can be broadly divided into failure-driven approaches and approaches that view acquisition as a by-product of processing. Here, we explore both approaches.

---

[12] Derived words, unlike inflected ones, have a different grammatical class than those of their stem (e.g. *work* vs. *worker*). On the other hand, inflected words have grammatical functions, and indicate, for example, whether a word has gender, is plural or possessive, etc. (*cat* vs. *cats*).

Autonomous Induction Theory

Failure-driven approaches propose that language learning is driven by processing failures and error detection such that the mechanisms responsible for acquisition are only activated when processing mechanisms fail (Schwartz, 1999; Wexler & Culicover, 1980). An example of one such approach is Susanne Carroll's (1999, 2001, 2007) Autonomous Induction Theory (AIT). AIT proposes that processing mechanisms fail when the learner's current system is unable to parse the input – that is, when the system cannot attribute an abstract representation to incoming linguistic stimuli. Instead of acknowledging the failure, the parser generates a best-fit solution to analyze the input. Whenever the parser cannot map form with meaning, a specialized learning procedure is activated.

With respect to the induction element of the AIT, Carroll makes an important distinction between inductive reasoning and inductive learning. Inductive reasoning takes place outside the language module and implicates the processing of conceptual structure, whereas inductive learning, which is not under conscious control, occurs within the language module and refers to "the novel encoding of information in a representation" (Carroll, 2001: 131). Similar to Fodor's (1998a, 1998b) Parsing-to-Learn Hypothesis, the AIT proposes that parsing relies on the same processing mechanisms regardless of whether the language in question is a first or a second language. In the case of second language acquisition, the same parsing procedures used in the first language are initially used to parse the second language – a procedure that inevitably results in failure at one point or another. This failure triggers the acquisition mechanisms. New parsing routines, based on the second language, are then constructed; these new routines must contend with pre-existing first language parsing routines, which are maintained until their activation thresholds are weak enough to be surpassed by second language parsing routines.

To illustrate, let's review an example. Imagine that a learner encounters the word "blik" in the context of *I saw the* ___ (Carroll, 2001: 135). In its attempt to classify the syntactic category of "blik," the learning mechanism is restricted to representations and classifications that could apply. If the learner's grammatical system has stored information regarding the high probability of a noun following the determiner *the*, the learning mechanism is likely to classify *blik* as a noun. English speakers know, however, that this information can be misleading because the article *the* can be followed by adverbs (e.g. *quite*) and adjectives (e.g. *small*). Thus, when learning English, the parser must decide among a Determiner+Noun, a Determiner+Adjective, or a Determiner+Adverb interpretation when faced with the utterance *the* + a novel form.

Parser as a Language Acquisition Device (PLAD)

Building on the notion of failure-driven learning and, more specifically, on Fodor's Parsing-to-Learn Hypothesis, Laurent Dekydtspotter and Claire Renaud (Dekydtspotter & Renaud, 2014) propose that the parser acts as the language acquisition device. A crucial assumption underlying this model is that the grammar is the interface between UG principles and the grammatical specifications encoded in the functional lexicon. Dekydtspotter and Renaud further argue that sentence processing is driven by "a parser that generates UG-sanctioned representations that must be licensed by language-specific information at each step" (Dekydtspotter & Renaud, 2014: 133). This language-specific information is expressed formally through the features encoded in functional categories and lexical items. Thus, parsing strategies can be viewed as the by-product of a language's grammatical specifications.

As discussed in work by Fodor (1998a, 1998b), grammatical learning is driven by the incremental parsing of input, where parsing failures enable the learner to apply the supergrammar and retrieve the most economical structure in order to represent the current input string. If we assume that the parser persistently assesses the success or failure of each structure it parses, it should follow that the structures that generate the most successful parses will be accessed more frequently, until the grammar adopts that structure. Such a process thus eliminates the need for an additional learning mechanism.

Dekydtspotter and Renaud (2014: 155) argue that the parser should be considered to be the language acquisition device, whereby the parser depends not only on the "incremental generation of UG-sanctioned representations," but also on the "licensing of these representations by an abstract parameterized lexicon". Thus, if a specific structure fails to generate a parse, the licensing conditions should hypothetically initiate the creation of new feature matrices of functional morphemes and other lexical items, leading to L2 linguistic knowledge growth. Within this framework, the L2 grammar acquisition mechanism is essentially the "parser embedded in the processing system" (Dekydtspotter & Renaud, 2014: 156).

We must, however, take into consideration that acquisition is incremental, characterized by stages that include periods of stability and change as new feature bundles become available. But why do stages occur? The incremental nature of learning may be explained by the way in which licensing works. For licensing to occur, the learner must access the relevant grammatical specifications from memory. Because working memory imposes restrictions on processing, accessing grammatical specifications must be done within a particularly narrow timeframe. Limited capacity models of second language processing suggest that cognitive resource constraints, such as working memory restrictions, can account for non-target-like second language processing (cf., Hopp, 2010; McDonald, 2006; Sorace, 2011). Stages in acquisition then arise as a result of the ever-changing relative strengths of activation, which stem from both licensing failures and successes during parsing. Learners' grammars thus undergo "a period of transition in which two values may be in competition" (Dekydtspotter & Renaud, 2014: 157).

To summarize, Dekydtspotter and Renaud argue that the PLAD initiates feature reassembly following processing failures in order to guide L2 learners in their transition from one state of grammatical knowledge to the next.

The Predictive Parser

Recently, several psycholinguists have proposed that anticipating linguistic information – a mechanism known as linguistic prediction – is one of the central mechanisms driving first language processing. Following this insight, Colin Phillips and Lara Ehrenhofer (Phillips & Ehrenhofer, 2015) propose that prediction also plays an important role in second language acquisition. According to them, learners can use their knowledge of the second language to parse a sentence and to predict how sentences will proceed. Predicting the upcoming word string before it unfolds would provide learners with valuable information that could help determine contingencies in language, as outlined in several models of language learning (e.g. Chang et al., 2006).

Phillips and Ehrenhofer discuss three ways in which learners' processing abilities can hinder or help second language acquisition. The first is that learners might simply not be able to parse sentences in real time. This possibility may not be as noxious because, if sentences cannot be parsed, learners cannot arrive at incorrect generalizations or representations, since there is nothing to represent or generalize. A second pitfall would be when learners mis-parse sentences, perhaps due to biases or a failure to reanalyze – a plausible finding even among first language speakers. This pitfall is potentially more damaging because learners could arrive at erroneous structural generalizations, or because learners could mis-parse the input even if it is both informative and clear. Why would this latter situation be the case? Because the input still goes through the filter of the learner's grammatical system to become intake.

The third consideration is that learners who can successfully parse a second language may vary in the amount of information they can extract from the sentences. But how can we know why learners vary? And how does this connect with predicting abilities? In Phillips and Ehrenhofer's view, this variation depends on predicting abilities, such that learners who can make more detailed and sophisticated predictions better learn complex language dependencies.

Furthermore, the authors suggest that learning is conditioned by learners' ability to perform a contrastive analysis between the predicted and actual input. Learners who passively analyze the input are able to identify what they can or cannot parse, but this information is only relevant for acquisition in the event of parsing failure. Learners who generate predictions, actively anticipating oncoming words and categories, have the potential to acquire more information about the linguistic input. When learners can assess the accuracy of their predictions, they can use feedback to either weaken or strengthen extant generalizations. Thus, Phillips and Ehrenhofer effectively consider the predictive parser to be a hypothesis-testing device.

The success of the predictive parser as a hypothesis-testing device depends on multiple factors. Proficiency might be a crucial one because beginning learners might not be able to both recognize and integrate the context cues in real time. Without this ability, learners cannot generate expectations. Moreover, an active learner can only really act on the feedback of predictions if these predictions are generated "quickly enough to 'get ahead of' the input" (Phillips & Ehrenhofer, 2015; 433). Our current understanding of how quickly predictions are generated is fairly limited, however, although early evidence shows that this might be a slow process.

At this point, we should raise a caveat to processing explanations. Previous research has shown that while children are highly successful language learners, they are not always good parsers (Snedeker & Trueswell, 2004). Adults, on the other hand, are generally said to be good at parsing, but do not always reach the same level of success as child learners. Phillips and Ehrenhofer propose two possibilities to account for these differences. The first is that adult learners are held back by their "deficits at other levels of language processing, such as sounds and words," since adult learners have been found to be much weaker in these areas, compared to children. It is possible that such deficits could be so detrimental that they may inhibit adults' overall parsing abilities (Phillips & Ehrenhofer, 2015: 440).

Such a possibility has been discussed by Holger Hopp (2018), who proposed the Lexical Bottleneck Hypothesis. The psycholinguistic literature provides evidence that language processing involves several distinct stages, which include lexical, syntactic, and semantic/discourse processing (Pickering & Gambi, 2018: 1002–1003). According to the Lexical Bottleneck Hypothesis, the first processing stage, lexical processing, gives rise to many of the difficulties that second language learners experience. More specifically, Hopp (2018: 13) argues that "the integrated nature of the bilingual mental lexicon with its core characteristics of weaker links and non-selective lexical access can yield input for syntactic processing that is less robust, more diffuse or delayed." Thus, problems in early stages of processing (i.e. lexical access) are likely to result in non-target syntactic processing.

The second possibility discussed by Phillips and Ehrenhofer is that both advanced adult and child learners have similar basic sentence processing abilities, but only adults are restricted by what they have previously learned. The authors suggest that adult learners' early successes restrict them to sentence processing routines that reduce their sensitivity to subsequent insights precisely because these routines are, initially, relatively successful, despite the fact that adult learners are not necessarily strong predictors at this stage. As learners become more advanced, and prediction becomes a more essential part of processing, adult second language learners are held back by their previously formed sentence-processing routines, which do not rely on prediction.

In sum, Phillips and Ehrenhofer (2015) do not see second language learners as fundamentally different from children processing their native language. The differences between the processing routines of both groups are, instead, attributed to lexical deficits and entrenched parsing routines.

Acquisition-by-Processing Theory

Michael Sharwood Smith and John Truscott have noted that while many generative transition theories have conceptualized second language learning in the form of failure-driven approaches, they offer an alternative approach via their Acquisition-by-Processing Theory (APT). Sharwood Smith and Truscott contend that acquisition should be conceptualized as "the lingering effects of processing" (Sharwood Smith & Truscott, 2014: 229). What do they mean by this? We will examine this view in more detail, but in a nutshell, they mean that acquisition is considered to be the by-product of processing itself, rather than the result of processing failure.

First, we depart from an observation highlighted by Sharwood Smith (2017: 88), who points out that acquisition is not typically characterized by "dramatic jumps"; instead, change occurs gradually. Accordingly, the APT suggests that acquisition (or "growth," as they call it) proceeds in a "a series of processing events" that occur within linguistic modules (Sharwood Smith & Truscott, 2014: 95). The first stage occurs when the processor encounters an unfamiliar string, but does not currently have access to the relevant representation in memory. What does the processor do, then? In response to this novel input, the processor of a specific linguistic module will construct a new structure online, by activating an item or items in working memory. This new structure will then persist in the memory store for a period of time, depending on how strongly it is activated. What regulates the strength of activation, according to these authors, is frequency. The more frequent a structure's usage, the higher its (resting) activation level. Thus, the activation level of a newly constructed form will be fairly low. This situation changes as the structure gradually gains or loses strength in response to incoming input. After time, provided that the form is sufficiently activated, the items are altered in long-term memory.

Superficially, the APT is not unlike some emergentist models in that it attributes a preeminent role to the input. However, the APT assumes that accessibility or retrievability of items in the memory is not directly modulated by the raw frequency structures in the input; instead, accessibility is regarded as a function of the activation within the module in question. Consequently, frequency of exposure will only influence a learner's linguistic development of some structure if it is processed by the relevant module(s). Thus, linguistic development is influenced by "the frequency of internal input to a given module and not the frequency of relevant events in the environment, the external input" (Truscott & Sharwood Smith, 2017: 905). Such an argument can therefore explain why the frequency of linguistic (external) input does not always reliably predict order of acquisition (Brown, 1973; Gass & Mackey, 2002).

5.4 Conclusion

In this section, we focused on transition theories of second language acquisition – theories that explain how learners progress from one state of linguistic knowledge to the next and that represent a number of recent GenSLA studies. These theories have been informed by seminal proposals, such as Fodor's Parsing-to-Learn Hypothesis, as well as by processing-based explanations that account for differences between first and second language processing, such as the SSH and RAGE hypotheses. Additionally, we reviewed how these recent avenues of GenSLA research place distinct emphases on the importance of failure-driven learning and error detection to explain the acquisition of new grammatical features. A notable exception is a proposal by Sharwood Smith and Truscott, which suggests that acquisition is a by-product of processing itself, rather than a by-product of processing failure. One thing is clear: second language researchers cannot talk about acquisition without considering language processing!

6 What Are the Key Readings?

6.1 A View of the Field via an Illustrative Study

In Sections 2 and 5, we discussed a number of different theories that, within a generative framework, attempt to explain second language development. Because of their influence in the field, we consider these to be among the key readings for any GenSLA neophyte. In this section, however, we aim to introduce other key readings and concepts by focusing on an illustrative GenSLA study that we believe provides us a view of the field (and where the field is going). To understand why this is the case, we must review a bit of history.

Within GenSLA, experimental methods have historically involved offline measures – tasks placing no time pressure on participants. These methods include grammaticality/acceptability judgment tasks and truth-value judgment tasks. This is because generative researchers have argued that, if designed appropriately, these tasks can tap into second language learners' underlying linguistic representations, although some researchers have noted that these tasks may encourage learners to rely on their metalinguistic knowledge to complete them (Bresnan, 2007; Schütze & Sprouse, 2014).

Offline methods are no longer a staple of the framework. An increasing number of researchers now use online methods, such as self-paced reading, eye-tracking, and event-related potentials (ERPs), to measure the moment-to-moment processing of various linguistic structures. In part, we can attribute this increase to the fact that online methods have become more accessible in terms of cost and ease of use. Another reason is that the researchers have shown a renewed interest in understanding how second language learners can compute linguistic representations during real-time processing. In fact, many of the more recent generative theories and hypotheses appeal to processing explanations to understand second language acquisition (Clahsen and Felser, 2006, 2018; Grüter et al, 2017). In this section, we explore this topic further by overviewing a study that we believe is representative of the current state of the science: Leal, Slabakova, and Farmer (2017).

We selected this article as an illustrative example for several reasons. First, this study is representative of the aforementioned change in the GenSLA research agenda, since it focuses squarely on the role that L2 learners' underlying linguistic representations play in the real-time processing of linguistic stimuli. It also echoes a number of generative processing-based studies that embrace cognitive constructs such as predictive processing and shallow structure processing, both of which are grounded in psycholinguistic theories. Second, the study focuses on a structure that has been found to be, for independent reasons, challenging for second language learners: Clitic Left Dislocation (CLLD) (Slabakova, Kempchinsky, & Rothman, 2012; Valenzuela, 2008). We mentioned CLLD as roughly equivalent to English topicalization in Section 3. CLLD is an interesting test case for theories of predictive processing because the presence of functional morphology (here, a clitic preceding a verb) depends not only on syntactic but also on discoursive information. As we have seen, there are hypotheses, such as the Interface Hypothesis (Sorace 2011), predicting that this acquisition is especially difficult. Finally, this study embodies another change within the generative tradition: the increasing interest in exploring the effects of input, in this case by studying the extent to which second language learners' exposure to the target language modulate their underlying linguistic development. While generative researchers have always considered input as a crucial element for acquisition, a renewed interest in the quantification of these effects is more recent.

6.2 What Is CLLD?

CLLD is a structure frequently used in Romance languages as a marker of topicalization, where a previously mentioned or discourse-salient phrase is reintroduced into the discourse by being moved, or dislocated, to the left of the sentence. Importantly, CLLD represents a long-distance syntactic dependency because the topicalized phrase that is moved to the left is linked to a piece of functional morphology: a clitic.

These dislocations cannot occur in any old discursive context, however. One of the requirements is that the dislocated phrase be a topic – something that has been previously mentioned in the discourse or else is easily retrievable from the context. For instance, if the noun phrase "the president" has been mentioned in the previous context, the following sentence is felicitous in Spanish (appearing in the Davies Spanish corpus, [Davies, 2019]).

(1) Al presidente   lo   elige el pueblo.
     to-the president   CL.masc.sing   chooses the people
     'The president   is elected   by the people.'

As is evident in the second line of this example, which represents the English word-by-word translation of the Spanish sentence, the phrase *The president* has moved to the left, all the way to the beginning of the sentence. Yet, this is not where we interpret said phrase – we still understand the sentence to mean that the people choose the president. Another very important characteristic of this particular dislocation is a little piece of morphology, which is marked as "CL" in the gloss. CL stands for clitic, or a piece of morphology that is phonologically dependent on another word. Because Spanish, like French in the examples we examined earlier, is a language with grammatical gender, we see that the clitic is masculine and singular to match the features of our dislocated phrase *el presidente*.

By now, we know this movement rule is not an arbitrary one, even in a relatively flexible language such as Spanish. Phrases that dislocate to the left in Spanish and that, moreover, are 'doubled' by a clitic, are typically topics.

Topics refer to "old information," or information that is easily retrievable in a given context. In Spanish, if the moved phrase is not old information, the clitic does not appear. To see how that works, let's place the previous sentence under a different context and see what changes:

(2)   Person A: The news said that only federal judges are chosen by the people.
       Person B: AL PRESIDENTE elige el pueblo (no a los jueces).
              to-the president chooses the people no to the judges
              'It is the president that the people elect (not the judges).'

To understand why the clitic pronoun vanished into thin air, we must examine the discourse context under which the sentence is embedded. Here, the phrase "the president" represents new information – information which also contradicts or corrects what Person A presented as fact (namely, that only judges are elected). Because the phrase is not a topic in this discursive context (instead, it represents new information, or what linguists call "Focus"), the clitic does not fit anymore.

6.3 Theoretical Grounding

Earlier, we reviewed hypotheses exploring how second language learners apply grammatical knowledge when they process language in real time. Two of the processing-based theories that we overviewed (the Shallow Structure Hypothesis and the Reduced Ability to Generate Expectations Hypothesis) are relevant for the present study, so we will mention them here. These hypotheses are both grounded in a generative theory of language, and they advance explicit predictions relating to second language learners' processing abilities. Since we have encountered these hypotheses before, we will only summarize their key tenets as they relate to the paper in question.

We saw that the Shallow Structure Hypothesis (SSH) (Clahsen & Felser, 2006, 2018) proposes that second language learners are unable to construct detailed syntactic representations of their second language. Why? The argument is that learners construct meaning exclusively by relying on lexical-semantic and/or pragmatic information, or on strategies that depend on argument structure. The SSH predicts that CLLD will be particularly challenging to acquire because learners have trouble processing long-distance dependencies, which rely on hierarchical syntactic relations (exactly the knowledge that learners are predicted not to have). Under the SSH, long-distance dependencies are also particularly challenging because second language speakers cannot rely on heuristic strategies to process them. Thus, evidence showing native-like processing of long-distance dependencies would be unexpected under the SSH. This would be the case even for advanced learners because the hypothesis explicitly rejects the notion that proficiency modulates processing patterns. In other words, the SSH predicts that we should not observe any development changes.

The second hypothesis we will revisit here is the RAGE hypothesis, which predicts that non-target-like behavior stems from the limited ability of second language learners to generate discourse-level expectations (Grüter et al., 2017). This is relevant to our discussion because CLLD is only felicitous in a specific discourse context: the dislocated material must have been previously mentioned for the clitic to appear. When this material is new information, the clitic does not appear. In the context of the current study, L2 speakers can only anticipate the clitic (the second element of the long-distance dependency) if they can integrate the discourse context. If second language speakers ignore the discourse context, they may associate the utterance with a clitic-less structure called Fronted Focus, which is also part of Spanish. Finally, the RAGE hypothesis does not explicitly link proficiency to a second language speaker's ability to predict upcoming information. Thus, evidence in line with this hypothesis should not show an effect of second language proficiency.

6.4 Aims of the Study

The study explores how CLLD is processed by second language learners and investigates whether second language proficiency can modulate the accuracy of predictions generated during processing. It also explores whether learners can predict the presence of a clitic before a main verb – a prediction that depends on the syntactic and discourse environment.

6.5 Research Methods

In addition to theoretical considerations, investigations grounded in generative theory must account for other factors, including considerations relating to the participants, research techniques, and experimental design. The illustrative study used a battery of tests that included a language background questionnaire, a proficiency test, a clitic-knowledge test, a self-paced reading task, and a sentence-norming task. In this section, we describe each task (in varying depth) and discuss how they contribute to the GenSLA research agenda.

6.5.1 Participants

Because generative linguists investigate how linguistic factors influence second language development, researchers pay close attention to the linguistic profiles of participants because the native language has been found to play a dominant role in modulating second language outcomes (Cho & Slabakova, 2014;

Domínguez, Arche, & Myles, 2017; Gil & Marsden, 2013; Guijarro-Fuentes, 2012; Hwang & Lardiere, 2013). In Leal et al. (2017), all 120 second language participants (members of what is called the "experimental" group) were native-English-speaking Spanish learners. By selecting participants from a single background, the authors were more easily able to exclude confounding factors.

Another important consideration is proficiency – especially when dealing with constructions that are known to be especially easy or difficult for learners. If a researcher studies a particularly easy construction, the data from very advanced learners might be less informative if they consistently perform at ceiling. Conversely, as shown in Leal et al. (2017), structures such as CLLD are challenging for second language learners on the level of both discourse and syntax. For this reason, the authors only selected participants who were beyond the very beginning stages of second language acquisition. If learners are unable to read the experimental items, there is little sense in testing their knowledge of syntax-discourse integration.

As a general rule, GenSLA studies also include what is known as a "control" group, typically comprised of native speakers of the target language, who represent the baseline of performance against which researchers compare second language learners. Control groups also validate the main test instruments. Our illustrative study included thirty-six monolingual speakers of Mexican Spanish who were of a similar socioeconomic background as the L2 learners. By including speakers from only one dialect of Spanish who come from similar socioeconomic backgrounds, the researchers avoided potential confounds relating to dialectal and/or socioeconomic differences that could impact linguistic performance (e.g., Pakulak & Neville, 2010).

Although native speaker data provide an interesting point of comparison and validation, researchers must exercise caution to avoid what is known as the 'comparative fallacy,' or directly comparing second language learners with monolingual L1 speakers (Bley-Vroman, 1983). Monika Schmid, Steven Gilbers, and Amber Nota quite pointedly note that if researchers compare learners with monolingual native speakers, one is "not only asking mere mortals [i.e. L2ers] to run as fast as Usain Bolt [i.e. monolingual natives], [one is] asking them to do so with lead weights [i.e. the L1] attached to their feet" (Schmid, Gilbers, & Nota, 2014: 152). As the linguist François Grosjean famously quipped, a bilingual is not two monolinguals rolled into one (Grosjean, 2008). In other words, second language learners, however proficient, will demonstrate an effect of bilingualism because they are, in fact, bilingual. To avoid the comparative fallacy, Leal and colleagues ran separate statistical analyses for native speakers and learners, only then comparing a sub-set of highly advanced learners with native speakers.

6.5.2 Experimental Instruments

Language Background Questionnaire and Proficiency Test

Controlling for participants' linguistic backgrounds constitutes a crucial factor. But how do researchers gather this information? As you might guess, studies typically include questionnaires and tests designed for this purpose. In this study, the authors included a language background questionnaire and an independent proficiency measure as part of their battery of tests. Although the proficiency test was not standardized, it did include excerpts from standardized tests and fifty multiple-choice items assessing vocabulary and grammar. Following other studies using the same measure (e.g. Slabakova et al., 2012), the authors considered scores between 40–50 to represent advanced learners, 25–39 intermediate learners, and below 25 beginner learners. The latter group was excluded from the study. This resulted in a total of 93 second language learners, including 56 of advanced proficiency and 37 of intermediate proficiency.

Clitic Knowledge Test

When conducting an experimental study, researchers must ensure the construct validity of the study – in short, that instruments measure what they are purported to measure. The acquisition of CLLD depends on syntactic and discourse knowledge, and part of this syntactic knowledge constitutes knowledge of the Spanish clitic system. This means learners need to know the syntactic properties of clitics before acquiring CLLD. To determine whether this was the case, the authors included a ten-item multiple-choice test, where learners could earn a maximum of fifty points, focused on the syntactic properties of clitics. If the authors had not determined this information before, it would have been impossible to know whether non-target-like results were attributable to inaccurate comprehension of CLLD or, rather, to lack of knowledge of clitics.

Sentence Norming Task

Our representative study aimed to investigate whether learners could anticipate the presence of a clitic based on contextual (discourse) restrictions. Note, however, that this aim presupposes that native speakers could also predict this piece of functional morphology: we cannot expect learners to demonstrate this ability if native speakers do not. In order to determine that native speakers did, in fact, conform to the expectations in the syntactic literature in this regard, the authors conducted what is known as a 'norming' sentence-completion task. This task was administered to a separate group of native speakers. It presented participants with a version of the experimental items that they were to complete. Each item included the contextual information, and the sentence up to where the clitic would be expected. This task thus allowed the researchers to determine, quantitatively, that native speakers did, in fact, anticipate the presence of the clitic, as predicted from the syntactic literature.

Self-Paced Reading Task

Because the representative study aimed to investigate processing, the authors chose a technique known as self-paced reading (SPR). In SPR tasks, participants read stimuli on a noncumulative segment-by-segment display, which is shown at a rate determined by the readers themselves (hence the term "self-paced") (Just, Carpenter, & Woolley, 1982). An underlying assumption of this technique is that reading times reflect participants' linguistic knowledge of a specific phenomenon by comparing their reaction times in two minimally different versions of a token. For this reason, many second language researchers have used this task to explore whether first and second language processing rely on fundamentally different mechanisms (Marsden, Thompson, & Plonsky, 2018).

Participants sat in front of a computer screen, where they were presented with a target sentence that followed a discourse context designed to ensure the felicity of CLLD (by introducing the topic). The test sentence was then presented in two minimally differing conditions: one where the clitic appeared before the main verb, as expected, and a second where the clitic was absent at that location, only to appear later on in the sentence. The latter condition was predicted to induce higher reading times because unexpected sentences are typically read at slower rates. Thus, slower reading times at the main verb would indicate that readers found the absence of the clitic unexpected; therefore, they processed it more slowly. Following the test sentence, participants were prompted to answer a Yes/No comprehension question. To avoid heuristic strategies when answering the questions, half of the comprehension questions focused on the context and the other half on the test sentence.

In total, the authors produced two versions of twenty-four test items, one where the clitic was present and one where the clitic was absent. The forty-eight test items were then counterbalanced across two presentation lists, such that each participant was exposed to twenty-four sentences per condition, or a version of each item. A further forty-eight sentences were included as distractors.

6.5.3 Analysis of Results

Over the years, data analysis techniques have grown in complexity (Loewen & Gass, 2009). In recent years, a number of researchers have suggested using mixed-effects regression models over the more commonly used ANOVAs (Cunnings, 2012; Linck & Cunnings, 2015). GenSLA researchers have followed suit, and mixed-effects models have gradually become the norm. Since mixed-effects models were used for the SPR data analysis in our representative study, we focus on those results.

Before running linear mixed-effects models on the dataset, the authors excluded data points with raw reading times greater than 5,000 ms or less than 100 ms; this procedure resulted in 1.5 percent of the data removed. Then, raw reading-time data were length-adjusted because it is well known that longer words take longer to read and that individuals differ in how long it takes them to read a given segment. This procedure followed an adapted version of the length-adjustment procedure advocated by Ferreira and Clifton (1986). Finally, the authors ran linear mixed-effects models, using maximal random effects structures (Barr et al., 2013). Maximal random effects structures include random intercepts and slopes for each fixed effect of interest to the study (Cunnings, 2012). These models were conducted using a package called lme4 (Bates et al., 2015) in the R environment (R Development Core Team, 2014), which is an open-source software.

Mixed-effects models offer GenSLA researchers a number of advantages because second language acquisition is affected by multiple variables (Cunnings, 2012). Mixed-effects models allow flexibility: researchers often focus on a combination of categorical and/or continuous independent variables – something mixed models can straight-forwardly handle. In this study, the clitic condition (absent, present) was included as a categorical variable,[13] while proficiency was treated as a continuous variable.[14] The fixed-effects dimension of a mixed-effects model allows the researcher to analyze these variables in parallel by including all the desired variables in a single model. In addition, researchers can also include interactions between variables; such inclusion offers the possibility of a general framework for analysis (Cunnings, 2012). In the representative study, the statistical analysis showed that both the main

---

[13] We can think of categorical (or discrete) variables as those that can result from counting. In a coin toss, the result can be either heads or tails – we can count the number of each outcome and these counts would constitute categorical values (e.g. 4 heads, 6 tails). Continuous variables, on the other hand, can assume any value in a continuum. When we measure time, the outcome measure is not limited to whole number values, such as 1 or 2 seconds; outcomes can assume value any value in between (e.g. 1.7298409 seconds).

[14] Whether proficiency should be coded as a categorical or continuous variable is an interesting question. We refer readers to Leal (2018a) for argumentation.

factors (clitic presence, proficiency) and their interaction produced significant results.

In addition to fixed effects, mixed-effects models can analyze random effects, allowing researchers to control for random variation (Linck & Cunnings, 2015). Because the representative study used what we call repeated measures (each participant produced multiple responses), two types of random effects were required. First, random intercepts modeled how each individual and/or test item's average reading time (regardless of experimental condition) differ. Second, random slopes allow researchers to gauge variability in sensitivity to the repeated measures' experimental manipulation (in this case, the clitic condition). In this study, the authors included a random slope for clitic condition on both the participant and item terms. It must be noted, however, that many researchers do not report the output from the random effects component of the model. The interested reader is encouraged to consult Barr et al. (2013) for further information on the subject.

6.6 Summary of findings

In this section, we presented an experimental study that we considered illustrative or representative of the current state of science in GenSLA. Briefly, the findings revealed that second language learners were sensitive to the violation of expectations that arose from the syntactic and discourse environment. Furthermore, this sensitivity varied as a function of proficiency: the more proficient the learner, the greater the reading time differences at the region of interest when the two clitic conditions (absent, present) were compared. At the most advanced levels of proficiency, learners were indistinguishable, statistically speaking, from native speakers. A particularly interesting result was that the size of the reading time differences was correlated with study abroad experience – not with years of study. Such a finding suggests that the quality of linguistic experience can modulate a learner's ability to accurately anticipate upcoming information during online processing.

As one could have guessed by now, these findings are unexpected if one espouses either the Shallow Structure Hypothesis or the RAGE hypothesis, both of which predict differences in processing patterns between native and second language speakers. However, second language learners showed evidence of generating expectations, even when said expectations involve discourse-level information and long-distance dependencies (hierarchical syntactic relations). Finally, this study underscored the effects of proficiency and study abroad, findings not predicted by either hypothesis.

6.7 A Note on the Importance of Offline Methods

Although we have focused predominantly on a study employing online methods, we must recognize the fundamental role that offline methods have played in the development of GenSLA as a discipline. Without the invaluable insights these offline methods have yielded, many discoveries would not have been made. For example, research by White and Genesee (1996) expanded our understanding of the end-state grammar. The authors of this study used a grammaticality judgment task to explore the sensitivity of UG to critical period effects and found native-like competency among L2 learners, even among post-critical-period learners.

Although production tasks have not been the prototypical choices of GenSLA researchers, these have been very useful sources of knowledge, especially in combination with judgment data. For example, spontaneous production data was used in Prévost and White (2000b) – a study that served as the basis for the Missing Surface Inflection Hypothesis. Prévost and White were interested in how French and German second language learners produced verbal agreement and finite and non-finite morphology. We mentioned earlier that production tasks are usually used in tandem with judgment tasks, but why would this be the case? First, as a general rule, we can say that data triangulation is preferable because, among other things, triangulation reduces bias (see Hoot, Leal, & Destruel, 2020). Additionally, GenSLA researchers have also argued that production data cannot provide us with the same level of insight as judgment data, in part because learners can avoid difficult structures or fail to produce structures that they can, in fact, produce. Thus, participants have wide latitude and selectively use structures in a way that might obscure their competence. Additionally, production tasks impose heightened computational loads because these occur in real time – a variable that might be challenging to control, depending on the aims of the study.

We must highlight that although online methods are increasingly common in GenSLA, these studies still represent a relatively small proportion of the literature at the present time. Finally, we conclude by highlighting that methods should be triangulated, to get a more accurate picture of the data.

6.8 Conclusion

We have presented a study we believe to be representative of the current state of science in the field of generative L2 acquisition. We saw how researchers have begun to use online methods, such as self-paced reading, to gain a deeper understanding of how second language learners represent linguistic knowledge. Additionally, this study explored psychological constructs such as prediction (anticipation) and studied whether learners could anticipate upcoming linguistic information when both syntactic and discourse information was involved. Finally, we reviewed methodological choices, using this study as a departure point. We highlighted that, as with any scientific endeavor, both the experimental design and data analysis play a crucial role in our interpretation.

References

Adjemian, C. (1976). On the Nature of Interlanguage Systems. *Language Learning*, 26(2), 297–320.

Barr, D. J., Levy, R., Scheepers, C., & Tily, H.J. (2013). Random Effects Structure for Confirmatory Hypothesis Testing: Keep It Maximal. *Journal of Memory and Language*, 68(3), 255–278.

Bates, D., Mächler, M., Bolker, B., & Walker, S. (2015). Fitting Linear Mixed-Effects Models Using lme4. *Journal of Statistical Software*, 67(1). doi:10.18637/jss.v067.i01

Belletti, A., Bennati, E., & Sorace, A. (2007). Theoretical and Developmental Issues in the Syntax of Subjects: Evidence from Near-Native Italian. *Natural Language & Linguistic Theory*, 25(4), 657–689.

Birdsong, D. (ed.). (1999). *Second Language Acquisition and the Critical Period Hypothesis*. Mahwah, New Jersey: Lawrence Erlbaum Associates.

Bley-Vroman, R. (1983). The Comparative Fallacy in Interlanguage Studies: The Case of Systematicity. *Language Learning*, 33(1),1–17.

Bloom, L. (1973). *One Word at a Time: The Use of Single Word Utterances*. The Hague: de Gruyter.

Borer, H. (1984). *Parametric Syntax: Case Studies in Semitic and Romance Languages*. Dordrecht: Foris Publications.

Bresnan, J. (2007). Is Syntactic Knowledge Probabilistic? Experiments with the English Dative Alternation. In S. Featherston & W. Sternefeld (eds.), *Roots: Linguistics in Search of Its Evidential Base*. Berlin: de Gruyter, pp. 77–96.

Brown, R. (1973). *A First Language*. Cambridge, MA: Harvard University Press.

Bybee, J. (2008). Usage-Based Grammar and Second Language Acquisition. In P. Robinson & N. Ellis (eds.), *Handbook of Cognitive Linguistics and Second Language Acquisition*. New York: Routledge, pp. 216–236.

Carroll, S. E. (1999). Putting "Input" in Its Proper Place. *Second Language Research*, **15**, 337–88.

Carroll, S. E. (2001). *Input and Evidence: The Raw Material of Second Language Acquisition* Amsterdam: John Benjamins.

Carroll, S. E. (2007). Autonomous Induction Theory. In B. VanPatten & J. Williams (eds.), *Theories in Second Language Acquisition*. Hillsdale, NJ: Lawrence Erlbaum Associates, pp. 155–200.

Carroll, S. E. (2017). Exposure and Input in Bilingual Development. *Bilingualism*, **20**(1), 3–16.

Chang, F., Dell, G. S. and Bock, K. (2006) 'Becoming syntactic.', *Psychological Review*, 113(2), pp. 234–272. doi: 10.1037/0033-295X.113.2.234.

Cho, J., & Slabakova, R. (2014). Interpreting Definiteness in a Second Language without Articles: The Case of L2 Russian. *Second Language Research*, **30**(2), 159–190.

Chomsky, N. (1957). *Syntactic Structures*. The Hague: Mouton de Gruyter.

Chomsky, N. (1965). *Aspects of the Theory of Syntax*. Cambridge: MIT Press.

Chomsky, N. (1981). *Lectures on Government and Binding*. Dordrecht: Foris.

Chomsky, N. (1995). *The Minimalist Program*. Cambridge: MIT Press.

Chomsky, N. (2001). Derivation by Phase. In M. Kenstowicz (ed.), *Ken Hale: A Life in Language*, Cambridge, MA: MIT Press, pp. 1–52.

Chomsky, N. (2005). Three Factors in Language Design. *Linguistic Inquiry*, **36** (1), 1–22.

Chomsky, N. (2013). Problems of Projection. *Lingua*, **130**, 33–49.

Clahsen, H., & Felser, C. (2006). Grammatical Processing in Language Learners. *Applied Psycholinguistics*, **27**(1), 3–42.

Clahsen, H., & Felser, C. (2018). Some Notes on the Shallow Structure Hypothesis. *Studies in Second Language Acquisition*, **40**(3), 693–706.

Clark, E. V. (2009). Lexical Meaning. In E. L. Bavin (ed.), *The Cambridge Handbook of Child Language*, New York: Cambridge University Press, pp. 283–300.

Clark, R. (1990). *Papers on learnability and natural selection: Technical reports on formal and computational linguistics, vol. 1.*

Clark, R., 1990. Papers on learnability and natural selection. *Technical reports in formal and computational linguistics, (Vol. 1)*. Universite de Geneve.

Clark, R. (1992). The Selection of Syntactic Knowledge. *Language Acquisition*, **2**, 83–149.

Cunnings, I. (2012). An Overview of Mixed-Effects Statistical Models for Second Language Researchers. *Second Language Research*, **28**(3), 369–382.

Cunnings, I. (2017). Parsing and Working Memory in Bilingual Sentence Processing. *Bilingualism: Language and Cognition*, **20**(4), 659–678.

Dallas, A. C. (2008). *Influences of Verbal Properties on Second-Language Filler-Gap Resolution: A Cross-Methodological Study*. Gainesville: University of Florida.

Davies, M. (2016). Corpus del Español: Two Billion Words, 21 Countries. www .corpusdelespanol.org/web-dial/.

Dekydtspotter, L., & Renaud, C. (2014). On Second Language Processing and Grammatical Development. *Linguistic Approaches to Bilingualism*, **4**(2), 131–165.

Dekydtspotter, L., Schwartz, B. D., & Sprouse, R. A. (2006). The Comparative Fallacy in L2 Processing Research. In M. G. O'Brien, C. Shea, & J. Archibald (eds.), *Proceedings of the 8th Generative Approaches to Second Language Acquisition Conference (GASLA 2006)*. Somerville, MA: Cascadilla Proceedings Project, pp. 33–40.

Domínguez, L., Arche, M. J., & Myles, F. (2017). Spanish Imperfect Revisited: Exploring L1 Influence in the Reassembly of Imperfective Features onto New L2 Forms. *Second Language Research*, **33**(4), 431–457.

Dussias, P. E., Valdés Kroff, J. R., Guzzardo Tamargo, R. E., & Gerfen, C. (2013). When Gender and Looking Go Hand in Hand: Grammatical Gender Processing in L2 Spanish. *Studies in Second Language Acquisition*, **35**(2), 353–387.

Eimas, P. D., Siqueland, E. R., Jusczyk, P., & Vigorito, J. (1971). Speech Perception in Infants. *Science*, **171**(3968), 303–306.

Ellis, N. (2002). Frequency Effects in Language Processing: A Review for Theories of Implicit and Explicit Language Acquisition. *Studies in Second Language Acquisition*, **24**, 143–188.

Elman, J. L., Bates, E. A., Johnson, M., Karmiloff-Smith, A., Parisi, D., & Plunkett, K. (1996). *Rethinking Innateness: A Connectionist Perspective on Development*, Cambridge, MA: MIT Press.

Epstein, S. D., Flynn, S., & Martohardjono, G. (1996). Second Language Acquisition: Theoretical and Experimental Issues in Contemporary Research. *Behavioral and Brain Sciences*, **19**(4), 677–714.

Felser, C., & Cunnings, I. (2012). Processing Reflexives in a Second Language: The Timing of Structural and Discourse-Level Constraints. *Applied Psycholinguistics*, **33**(3), 571–603.

Felser, C., Roberts, L., Marinis, T., & Gross, R. (2003). The processing of ambiguous sentences by first and second language learners of English. Applied Psycholinguistics, 24(3), 453–489.

Ferreira, F., & Clifton, C. (1986). The Independence of Syntactic Processing. *Journal of Memory and Language*, **25**(3), 348–368.

Flynn, S. (1985). Principled Theories of L2 Acquisition. *Studies in Second Language Acquisition*, **7**(1), 99–108.

Fodor, J. D. (1998a). Leaning to Parse? *Journal of Psycholinguistic Research*, **27**(2), 285–319.

Fodor, J. D. (1998b). Parsing to Learn. *Journal of Psycholinguistic Research*, **27**(3), 339–374.

Fodor, J. D., & Sakas, W. (2017). Learnability. In I. Roberts (ed.), *The Oxford Handbook of Universal Grammar*. Oxford: Oxford University Press, pp. 249–269.

Fukui, N. (1988). Deriving the differences between English and Japanese: A case study in parametric syntax. *English Linguistics*, **5**, 249–270.

Granena, G., & Long, M. (eds.). (2013). *Sensitive Periods, Language Aptitude, And Ultimate L2 Attainment*. Amsterdam: John Benjamins.

Gass, S. M. (1988). Integrating Research Areas: A Framework for Second Language Studies, *Applied Linguistics*, 19, 198–217.

Gass, S. M., & Mackey, A. (2002). Frequency Effects and Second Language Acquisition. *Studies in Second Language Acquisition*, **24**(2), 249–260.

Gibson, T., & Wexler, K. (1994). Triggers. *Linguistic Inquiry*, **25**, 407–454.

Gil, K.-H., & Marsden, H. (2013). Existential Quantifiers in Second Language Acquisition. *Linguistic Approaches to Bilingualism*, **3**(2), 117–149.

Goldberg, A. E. (2006). *Constructions at Work: The Nature of Generalization in Language*, Oxford: Oxford University Press.

Gregg, K. R. (2003). The State of Emergentism in Second Language Acquisition. *Second Language Research*, **19**(2), 95–128.

Grüter, T., Rohde, H., & Schafer, A. J. (2017). Coreference and Discourse Coherence in L2. *Linguistic Approaches to Bilingualism*, **7**(2), 199–229.

Guijarro-Fuentes, P. (2012). The Acquisition of Interpretable Features in L2 Spanish: Personal a. *Bilingualism: Language and Cognition*, **15**(04), 701–720.

Halberda, J. (2003). The Development of a Word-Learning Strategy. *Cognition*, **87**(1), B23–B34.

Hart, B., & Risley, T. (1995). *Meaningful Differences in the Everyday Lives of American Children*, Baltimore, MD: Brookes Publishing.

Hart, B., & Risley, T. (1999). *The Social World of Children Learning to Talk*. Baltimore: Paul H. Brookes Publishing.

Hawkins, R., & Casillas, G. (2008). Explaining Frequency of Verb Morphology in Early L2 Speech. *Lingua*, **118**(4), 595–612.

Hawkins, R., & Chan, C. Y.-H. (1997). The PaAtial availability of Universal Grammar in Second Language Acquisition: The 'Failed Functional Features Hypothesis.' *Second Language Research*, **13**(3), 187–226.

Haznedar, B. (1997). L2 Acquisition by a Turkish-Speaking Child: Evidence for L1 Influence. In E. Hughes, M. Hughes, & A. Greenhill (eds.), *Proceedings of the 21st Annual Boston University Conference on Language Development*, Somerville, MA: Cascadilla Press, pp. 257–268.

Haznedar, B. (2001). The Acquisition of the IP System in Child L2 English. *Studies in Second Language Acquisition*, **23**(1), 1–39.

Haznedar, B., & Schwartz, B. D. (1997). Are There Optional Infinitives in Child L2 Acquisition? In E. Hughes, M. Hughes, & A. Greenhill (eds.), *Proceedings of the 21st Annual Boston University Conference on Language Development*, Somerville, MA: Cascadilla Press., pp. 257–268.

Hoff, E., & Naigles, L. (2002). How Children Use Input to Acquire a Lexicon. *Child Development*, **73**(2), 418–433.

Holmberg, A., & Roberts., I. (2014). Parameters and the three factors of language design. In M. C. Picallo (ed.), *Linguistic Variation in the Minimalist Framework*, Oxford: Oxford University Press, pp. 61–81.

Hoot, B., Leal, T., & Destruel, E. (2020). Object focus marking in Spanish: An investigation using three tasks. Glossa: a journal of general linguistics, 5(1): 70. 1–32. DOI: https://doi.org/10.5334/gjgl.1160

Hopp, H. (2010). Ultimate Attainment in L2 Inflection: Performance Similarities between Non-native and Native Speakers. *Lingua*, **120**(4), 901–931.

Hopp, H. (2013). Grammatical Gender in Adult L2 Acquisition: Relations between Lexical and Syntactic Variability. *Second Language Research*, **29** (1), 33–56.

Hopp, H. (2018). The bilingual mental lexicon in L2 sentence processing, Second Language, 17, 5–27.

Hwang, S. H., & Lardiere, D. (2013). Plural-Marking in L2 Korean: A Feature-Based Approach. *Second Language Research*, **29**(1), 57–86.

Hymes, D. (1972). On Communicative Competence. In J. Pride & J. Holmes (eds.), *Sociolinguistics*, Harmondsworth, UK: Penguin Books, pp. 269–293.

Jensen, I., Slabakova, R., Westergaard, M., & Lundquist, B. (2020). The Bottleneck Hypothesis in L2 Acquisition: L1 Norwegian Learners' Knowledge of Syntax and Morphology in L2 English. *Second Language Research* **36**(1), 3–29.

Just, M. A., Carpenter, P. A., & Woolley, J.D. (1982). Paradigms and Processes in Reading Comprehension. *Journal of Experimental Psychology: General*, **111**(2), 228–238.

Kaan, E., Dallas, A. C., & Wijnen, F. (2010). Syntactic Predictions in Second-Language Sentence Processing. In J.-W. Zwart & M. de Vries (eds.), *Structure Preserved: Festschrift in the Honor of Jan Koster*. Amsterdam: John Benjamins, pp. 207–2013.

Kanno, K. (1997). The Acquisition of Null and Overt Pronominals in Japanese by English Speakers. *Second Language Research*, **13**(3), 265–287.

Krashen, S. (1982). *Principles and Practice in Second Language Acquisition*, Oxford: Pergamon.

Kwon, S.-N., & Zribi-Hertz, A. (2004). Number from a Syntactic Perspective: Why Plural Marking Looks 'Truer' in French than in Korean. In O. Bonami & P. C. Hofherr (eds.), *Empirical Issues in Formal Syntax and Semantics 5*, pp. 133–158.

Lardiere, D. (1998a). Case and Tense in the 'Fossilized' Steady State. *Second Language Research*, **14**(1), 1–26.

Lardiere, D. (1998b). Dissociating Syntax from Morphology in a Divergent L2 End-State Grammar. *Second Language Research*, **14**(4), 359–375.

Lardiere, D. (2009). Some Thoughts on the Contrastive Analysis of Features in Second Language Acquisition. *Second Language Research*, **25**(2), 173–227.

Leal, T. (2018a). Data Analysis and Sampling: Methodological Issues Concerning Proficiency in SLA Research. In A. Edmonds & A. Gudmestad (eds.), *Critical Reflections on Data in Second Language Acquisition*, Amsterdam: John Benjamins, pp. 63–88.

Leal, T. (2018b). Mapping at External Interfaces: Embedded Clitic Left Dislocations in L2 Spanish. In J. Cho, M. Iverson, T. Judy, T. Leal, & E. Shimanskaya (eds.), *Meaning and Structure in Second Language Acquisition: In Honor of Roumyana Slabakova*, Amsterdam: John Benjamins, pp. 36–65.

Leal, T., & Slabakova, R. (2019). The Relationship between L2 Instruction, Exposure, and the L2 Acquisition of a Syntax–Discourse Property in L2 Spanish. *Language Teaching Research*, **23**(2), 237–258.

Leal, T., Slabakova, R., & Farmer, T. A. (2017). The Fine-Tuning of Linguistic Expectations over the Course of L2 learning. *Studies in Second Language Acquisition*, **39**(3), 493–525.

Lee, E., & Lardiere, D. (2019). Feature Reassembly in the Acquisition of Plural Marking by Korean and Indonesian Bilinguals. *Linguistic Approaches to Bilingualism*, **9**(1), 73–119.

Lewis, S., & Phillips, C. (2014). Aligning Grammatical Theories and Language Processing Models. *Journal of Psycholinguistic Research*, **44**(1), 27–46.

Liceras, J. (1986). *Linguistic Theory and Second Language Acquisition: The Spanish Nonnative Grammar of English Speakers*, Tübingen: Günter Narr.

Liceras, J. M., Zobl, H., & Goodluck, H. (2008). *The Role of Formal Features in Second Language Acquisition*, New York: Routledge.

Lidz, J., & Gagliardi, A. (2015). How Nature Meets Nurture: Universal Grammar and Statistical Learning. *Annual Review of Linguistics*, **1**(1), 333–353.

Lightfoot, D. (1991). *How to Set Parameters*, Cambridge: MIT Press.

Lightfoot, D. (1999). *The Development of Language: Acquisition, Change and Evolution*, Cambridge: Wiley-Blackwell.

Linck, J. A., & Cunnings, I. (2015). The Utility and Application of Mixed-Effects Models in Second Language Research. *Language Learning*, **65**(S1), 185–207.

Loewen, S., & Gass, S. (2009). The Use of Statistics in L2 Acquisition Research. *Language Teaching*, **42**(2), 181–196.

Marinis, T., Roberts, L., Felser, C., & Clahsen, H. (2005). Gaps in Second Language Sentence Processing. *Studies in Second Language Acquisition*, **27**(1), 53–78.

Marsden, E., Thompson, S., & Plonsky, L. (2018). A Methodological Synthesis of Self-Paced Reading in Second Language Research. *Applied Psycholinguistics*, **39**(5), 861–904.

Marsden, H. (2009). Distributive Quantifier Scope in English-Japanese and Korean-Japanese Interlanguage. *Language Acquisition*, **16**(3), 135–177.

Martohardjono, G. (1993). *Wh-movement in the Acquisition of a Second Language: A Cross-Linguistic Study of Three Languages with and without Movement*, Cornell University.

McDonald, J. L. (2006). Beyond the Critical Period: Processing-Based Explanations for Poor Grammaticality Judgment Performance by Late Second Language Learners. *Journal of Memory and Language*, **55**(3), 381–401.

Mitchell, R., Myles, F., & Marsden, E. (2013). *Second Language Learning Theories*, New York: Routledge.

O'Grady, W. (2005). *How Children Learn Language*, Cambridge: Cambridge University Press.

Papadopoulou, D., & Clahsen, H. (2003). Parsing strategies in L1 and L2 sentence processing: A study of relative clause attachment in Greek. Studies in Second Language Acquisition, 501–528.

Pearl, L. S., & Lidz, J. (2009). When Domain General Learning Fails and When It Succeeds: Identifying the Contribution of Domain Specificity. *Language Learning and Development*, **5**, 235–65.

Phillips, C., & Ehrenhofer, L. (2015). The Role of Language Processing in Language Acquisition. *Linguistic Approaches to Bilingualism*, **5**(4), 409–453.

Pienemann, M. (1998). *Language Processing and Second Language Development: Processability Theory*. Amsterdam: John Benjamins.

Pinker, S. (1989). *Learnability and Cognition*, Cambridge, MA: MIT Press.

Pliatsikas, C., & Marinis, T. (2013). Processing Empty Categories in a Second Language: When Naturalistic Exposure Fills the (Intermediate) Gap. *Bilingualism: Language and Cognition*, **16**(1), 167–182.

Prévost, P., & White, L. (2000a). Accounting for Morphological Variation in Second Language Acquisition: Truncation of Missing Inflection? In M.-A. Friedemann & L. Rizzi (eds.), *The Acquisition of Syntax*, London: Longman, pp. 202–235.

Prévost, P., & White, L. (2000b). Missing Surface Inflection or Impairment in second language acquisition?: Evidence from tense and agreement. *Second Language Research*, **16**(2), 103–133.

R Core Development Team (2014) 'R: A language and environment for statistical computing.' Vienna, Austria: R Foundation for Statistical Computing. Available at: http://www.rproject.org.

Rankin, T., & Unsworth, S. (2016). Beyond Poverty: Engaging with Input in Generative SLA. *Second Language Research*, **32**(4), 563–572.

Rastelli, S., & Gil, K. H. (2018). No Fear of George Kingsley Zipf: Language Classroom, Statistics and Universal Grammar. *Instructed Second Language Acquisition*, **2**(2), 242–264.

Regier, T., & Gahl, S. (2003). Learning the Unlearnable: The Role of Missing Evidence. *Cognition*, **93**, 147–55.

Roehr-Brackin, K. (2015). Explicit knowledge about language in L2 learning: A usage-based perspective. In P. Rebuschat (Ed.), *Implicit and explicit learning of languages* (pp. 117–138). John Benjamins Publishing Company.

Rothman, J., & Slabakova, R. (2018). The Generative Approach to SLA and Its Place in Modern Second Language Studies. *Studies in Second Language Acquisition*, **40**(2), 417–442.

Saffran, J. R. (2003). Statistical Language Learning. *Current Directions in Psychological Science*, **12**(4), 110–114.

Sagarra, N., & Herschensohn, J. (2013). Processing of Gender and Number Agreement in Late Spanish Bilinguals. *International Journal of Bilingualism*, **17**(5), 607–627.

Schachter, J. (1988). Second Language Acquisition and Its Relationship to Universal Grammar. *Applied Linguistics*, **9**(3), 219–235.

Schmid, M. S., Gilbers, S., & Nota, A. (2014). Ultimate Attainment in Late Second Language Acquisition: Phonetic and Grammatical Challenges in Advanced Dutch–English Bilingualism. *Second Language Research*, **30**(2), 129–157.

Schütze, C. T., & Sprouse, J. (2014). Judgment Data. In R. J. Podesva & D. Sharma (eds.), *Research Methods in Linguistics*, Cambridge: Cambridge University Press, pp. 27–50.

Schwartz, B. D. (1999). Let's Make up Your Mind: "Special Nativist" Perspectives on Language, Modularity of Mind, and Nonnative Language Acquisition. *Studies in Second Language Acquisition*, **21**, 635–55.

Schwartz, B., & Gubala-Ryzak, M. (1992). Learnability and Grammar Reorganization in L2A: Against Negative Evidence Causing the unlearning of verb movement. *Second Language Research*, **8**(1), 1–38.

Schwartz, B. D., & Sprouse, R. A. (1994). Word Order and Nominative Case in Nonnative Language Acquisition: A Longitudinal Study of (L1 Turkish) German Interlanguage. In T. Hoekstra & B. D. Schwartz (eds.), *Language Acquisition Studies in Generative Grammar*, Amsterdam: John Benjamins, pp. 317–368.

Schwartz, B. D., & Sprouse, R. A. (1996). L2 Cognitive States and the Full Transfer/Full Access Model. *Second Language Research*, **12**(1), 40–72.

Schwartz, B. D. & Sprouse, R. (2013). Generative approaches and the Poverty of the Stimulus. In J. Herschensohn and M. Young-Scholten (eds), *The Cambridge handbook of Second Language Acquisition*. Cambridge: Cambridge University Press, pp. 137–58.

Sharwood Smith, M. (2017). *Introducing Language and Cognition*, Cambridge: Cambridge University Press. doi:10.1017/9781316591505

Sharwood Smith, M., & Truscott, J. (2014). *The Multilingual Mind: A Modular Processing Perspective*, Cambridge: Cambridge University Press.

Shimanskaya, E. (2015). *Feature Reassembly of Semantic and Morphosyntactic Pronominal Features in L2 Acquisition*, University of Iowa.

Shimanskaya, E. (2018). On the Role of Input in Second Language Acquisition: The Case of French Strong Pronouns. *Language Learning*, **68**(3), 780–812.

Slabakova, R. (2000). L1 Transfer Revisited: The L2 Acquisition of Telicity Marking in English by Spanish and Bulgarian Native Speakers. *Linguistics*, **38**(4), 739–770.

Slabakova, R. (2002). The Compounding Parameter in Scond Language Acquisition. *Studies in Second Language Acquisition*, **24**(4), 507–540.

Slabakova, R. (2005). What Is So Difficult about Telicity Marking in L2 Russian? *Bilingualism: Language and Cognition*, **8**(1), 63–77.

Slabakova, R. (2006). Is There a Critical Period for Semantics? *Second Language Research*, **22**(3), 302–338.

Slabakova, R. (2008). *Meaning in the Second Language*, New York/Berlin: Mouton de Gruyter.

Slabakova, R. (2015). The Effect of Construction Frequency and Native Transfer on Second Language Knowledge of the Syntax–Discourse Interface. *Applied Psycholinguistics*, **36**(3), 671–699.

Slabakova, R. (2016). *Second Language Acquisition*, Oxford: Oxford University Press.

Slabakova, R., Kempchinsky, P., & Rothman, J. (2012). Clitic-Doubled Left Dislocation and Focus Fronting in L2 Spanish: A Case of Successful Acquisition at the Syntax–Discourse Interface. *Second Language Research*, **28**(3), 319–343.

Slabakova, R., Leal, T., & Liskin-Gasparro, J. (2014). We Have Moved On: Current Concepts and Positions in Generative SLA. *Applied Linguistics*, **35**(5), 601–606.

Slabakova, R., Leal, T., & Liskin-Gasparro, J. (2015). Rumors of UG's Demise Have Been Greatly Exaggerated. *Applied Linguistics*, **36**(2), 265–269.

Snyder, W. (2001). On the Nature of Syntactic Variation: Evidence from Complex Predicates and Complex Word-Formation. *Language*, **77**(2), 324–342.

Sorace, A. (2011). Pinning down the Concept of "Interface" in Bilingualism. *Linguistic Approaches to Bilingualism*, **1**(1), 1–33.

Tenenbaum, J. B., & Griffiths, T. L. (2001). Generalization, Similarity, and Bayesian Inference. *Behavioral and Brain Sciences*, **24**, 629–40.

Thordardottir, E. (2015). The Relationship between Bilingual Exposure and Morphosyntactic Development. *International Journal of Speech-Language Pathology*, **17**(2), 97–114.

Tomasello, M. (2000). Do Young Children have Adult Syntactic Competence? *Cognition*, **74**(3), 209–253.

Tomasello, M. (2003). *Constructing a Language: A Usage-Based Theory of Language Acquisition*. Cambridge, MA: Harvard University Press.

Truscott, J., & Sharwood Smith, M. (2017). Representation, Processing and Code-Switching. *Bilingualism: Language and Cognition*, **20**(5), 903–916.

Tsimpli, I. M., & Dimitrakopoulou, M. (2007). The Interpretability Hypothesis: Evidence from *wh*-interrogatives in Second Language Acquisition. *Second Language Research*, **23**(2), 215–242.

Unsworth, S. (2016). Early Child L2 Acquisition: Age or Input Effects? Neither, or Both? *Journal of Child Language*, **43**(3), 608–634.

Vainikka, A., & Young-Scholten, M. (1994). Direct Access to X'-Theory: Evidence from Korean and Turkish Adults Learning German. In T. Hoekstra & B. Schwartz (eds.), *Language Acquisition Studies in Generative Grammar*, Amsterdam: John Benjamins, pp. 31–48.

Valenzuela, E. (2008). L2 End State Grammars and Incomplete Acquisition of Spanish CLLD Constructions. In R. Slabakova, S. A. Montrul, & P. Prévost (eds.), *Inquiries in Linguistic Development: In honor of Lydia White*, Amsterdam: John Benjamins, pp. 283–304.

van Gompel, R. P. G., & Pickering, M. J. (2007). Syntactic Parsing. In M. G. Gaskell (ed.), *The Oxford Handbook of Psycholinguistics*, Oxford: Oxford University Press, pp. 289–307.

VanPatten, B. (1996). *Input Processing and Grammar Instruction in Second Language Acquisition*. Norwood: Ablex.

Viau, J., & Lidz, J. (2011). Selective Learning in the Acquisition of Kannada Ditransitives. *Language*, **87**(4), 679–714.

Vikner, S. (1995) *Verb Movement and Expletive Subjects in the Germanic Languages*. Oxford and New York: Oxford University Press.

Weerman, F. (1989). The V2 conspiracy: A synchronic and a diachronic analysis of verbal positions in Germanic languages. Dordrecht: Foris.

Westergaard, M. & Vangsnes, Ø. A. (2005) Wh-questions, V2, and the Left Periphery of Three Norwegian Dialects. *Journal of Comparative Germanic Linguistics*, **8**, 117–158.

Wexler, K., & Culicover, P. W. (1980). *Formal Principles of Language Acquisition*, Cambridge, MA: MIT Press.

White, L. (1985). The "Pro-drop" Parameter in Adult Second Language Acquisition. *Language Learning*, **35**(1), 47–61.

White, L. (1987). Against Comprehensible Input: The Input Hypothesis and the Development of Second-language Competence. *Applied Linguistics*, **8**(2), 95–110.

White, L. (1989). *Universal Grammar and Second Language Acquisition*, Amsterdam: John Benjamins.

White, L. (1991). Adverb Placement in Second Language Acquisition: Some Effects of Positive and Negative Evidence in the Classroom. *Second Language Research*, **7**(2), 133–161.

White, L. (2003). *Second Language Acquisition and Universal Grammar*, Cambridge: Cambridge University Press.

White, L. (2018a). Formal Linguistics and Second Language Acquisition. In D. Miller, F. Bayram, J. Rothman, & L. Serratrice (eds.), *Bilingual Cognition and Language: The State of the Acience across Its Subfields*, Amsterdam: John Benjamins, pp. 57–77.

White, L. (2018b). What Is Easy and What Is Hard: Lessons from Linguistic Theory and SLA Research. In J. Cho, M. Iverson, T. Judy, T. Leal, & E. Shimanskaya (eds.), *Meaning and Structure in Second Language Acquisition: In Honor of Roumyana Slabakova*, Amsterdam: John Benjamins, pp. 263–282.

White, L., & Genesee, F. (1996). How Native is Near-Native? The Issue of Ultimate Attainment in Adult Second Language Acquisition. *Second Language Research*, **12**(3), 233–265.

White, L., & Juffs, A. (1998). Constraints on Wh- Movement in Two Different Contexts of Non-Native Language Acquisition: Competence and Processing. In S. Flynn, G. Martohardjono, & W. O'Neill (eds.), *The Generative Study of Second Language Acquisition*, Hillsdale, NJ: Lawrence Erlbaum Associates, pp. 111–130.

White, L., Valenzuela, E., Kozlowska-Macgregor, M., & Leung, Y.I . (2004). Gender and Number Agreement in Nonnative Spanish. *Applied Psycholinguistics*, **25**(1), 105–133.

Whong, M., Gil, K.-H., & Marsden, H. (eds.). (2013). *Universal Grammar and the Second Language Classroom*, New York: Springer.

Yang, C. (2002). *Knowledge and Learning in Natural Language*, Oxford: Oxford University Press.

Yang, C. (2004). Universal Grammar, Statistics or Both? *Trends in Cognitive Sciences*, **8**(10), 451–456.

Yang, C. (2012). Computational Models of Syntactic Acquisition. *Wiley Interdisciplinary Reviews: Cognitive Science*, **3**(2), 205–213.

Yang, C. (2018). A Formalist Perspective on Language Acquisition. *Linguistic Approaches to Bilingualism*, **8**(6), 665–706.

Second Language Acquisition

Alessandro Benati

The University of Hong Kong

Alessandro Benati is Director of CAES at The University of Hong Kong (HKU). He is known for his work in second language acquisition and second language teaching. He has published ground-breaking research on the pedagogical framework called Processing Instruction. He is co-editor of a new online series for Cambridge University Press, a member of the REF Panel 2021, and Honorary Professor at York St John University.

John W. Schwieter

Wilfrid Laurier University, Ontario

John W. Schwieter is Associate Professor of Spanish and Linguistics, and Faculty of Arts Teaching Scholar, at Wilfrid Laurier University. His research interests include psycholinguistic and neurolinguistic approaches to multilingualism and language acquisition; second language teaching and learning; translation and cognition; and language, culture, and society.

About the Series

Second Language Acquisition showcases a high-quality set of updatable, concise works that address how learners come to internalize the linguistic system of another language and how they make use of that linguistic system. Contributions reflect the interdisciplinary nature of the field, drawing on theories, hypotheses, and frameworks from education, linguistics, psychology, and neurology, among other disciplines. Each Element in this series addresses several important questions: What are the key concepts?; What are the main branches of research?; What are the implications for SLA?; What are the implications for pedagogy?; What are the new avenues for research?; and What are the key readings?

Cambridge Elements ⁼

Second Language Acquisition

Elements in the Series

Printed in the United States
By Bookmasters